Just Jesus

The Evidence of History

James T. South, Ph.D.

DEWARD
PUBLISHING COMPANY

Just Jesus: The Evidence of History
© 2012 by DeWard Publishing Company, Ltd.
P.O. Box 6259, Chillicothe, Ohio 45601
800.300.9778
www.deward.com

Cover design by Jonathan Hardin.

Any emphasis in Bible quotations is added.

Printed in the United States of America.

ISBN: 978-1-936341-42-9

To Stacy, Kurt, and Kent

With gratitude for the joy of being their earthly father.
"Behold, children are a heritage from the Lord" (Psa 127.3).

Contents

Introduction:
"Why Another Book about Jesus?"

Anyone who has ever browsed through the Religion section of almost any bookstore knows there are already lots of books about Jesus, and new ones are appearing all the time. They are written from all sorts of perspectives—some skeptical, some believing—and many of them are written in reaction to one another. In addition, various news magazines frequently feature articles about Jesus, about supposed new discoveries about him, and the latest religious squabbles about who he was and what he did and said.

That raises a valid question: Why another book about Jesus? Why add this one to the already lengthy list of what's available? It's a fair question, and I'll try to give a fair answer.

First, a lot of what has been written about Jesus isn't historically based. People are interested in Jesus—in almost anything anyone says about Jesus—and so publishers rush things into print that may not have much validity. Some authors write from a biased point of view that causes other writers and scholars (yes, even scholars!) to say things that aren't historically verifiable or to draw faulty conclusions from historical evidence. Also, there seems to be a strong public taste for the sensational, and publishers seem eager to feed it. As Ben Witherington III has well put it,

> We live in a Jesus-haunted culture that is biblically illiterate. ...
> In this sort of environment, almost any wild theory about Jesus
> or his earliest followers can pass for knowledge with some audi-
> ences, because so few people actually know the primary sources,

the relevant texts, or the historical context with which we should be concerned. In our soap opera culture, perhaps it was inevitable that someone would turn the story of Jesus into a soap opera.[1]

So there remains a need to cut through all of the theories in the interest of historical accuracy, and this is what I hope to accomplish in this small book.

Second, much of the historical information that is available about Jesus is not readily accessible to the general public. Those who are sincerely interested in Jesus often end up buying and reading books that may be misleading because they're available and they're readable. For example, the various non-biblical sources that mention Jesus have been known for a long time, if you know where to look. But most people don't know. This book offers that information in a format and in language that is easily accessible. That's why you won't find an overload of footnotes here, just enough to point you in the right direction in case you want to know more, but not so many that you'll be overwhelmed.

Third, both secular and religious approaches to Jesus sometimes treat him as if he were not a real person. Skeptics dismiss him as either never having existed or as being nothing like the New Testament describes him. Believers sometimes discuss him in a historical and cultural vacuum, as if he could have lived at any time and any place and our understanding of him wouldn't be affected at all. But Jesus was real, according to all of the ancient sources. And as a real person, there is much we can know about his life that is often overlooked. This book tries not to overlook it.

Fourth, I offer another book on Jesus because those of us who believe in him and teach about him in academic and religious settings are of the opinion that no one can know too much about him and most people don't know nearly enough. If the publication of one more book will cause people to examine the evidence and learn about Jesus for themselves, then it's well worth the effort. It's my prayer that you'll be one of those people.

Before going further, I'd like to express my appreciation to all

---

[1]Ben Witherington III, *What Have They Done With Jesus? Beyond Strange Theories and Bad History—Why We Can Trust the Bible* (HarperCollins, 2007), 2.

of my students, past and present, who sat through my classes on "New Testament Introduction" and "Jesus in the New Testament" at Virginia Commonwealth University, and to the members of the Glen Allen Church of Christ in Glen Allen, Virginia. I developed this material originally for them and it has been shaped to some extent by their questions and concerns. I hope they found it helpful, and I hope you will, too.

Preface

Whether you believe in Jesus or not, you have to admit he's a fascinating character. He must be, since people seem unable to ignore him. He has his devotees and his detractors, but few people are neutral about Jesus.

And yet, how much do people really *know* about Jesus? How much do *you* know? It only makes sense that whether we're going to follow him or denounce him, we ought to at least know what and who we're talking about.

That's what this book is about: what we can (and, to some extent, can't) know about Jesus. Jesus isn't just a religious idea but a phenomenon of history. That means we can and should ask about him all of the historical questions we can think of and see which ones can and can't be answered. Fortunately, we're able to learn a lot more about Jesus than most people think.

I realize that, for many, the words "Jesus" and "history" just don't go together. Some think of him only in the realm of a religious belief for which history is irrelevant, and others are convinced nothing truly historical can be known about him. But the sources at our disposal lead us to think otherwise. They point to a Jesus who lived at a certain point in history, in a particular geographical location, and in a readily identifiable cultural milieu—all of which suggests that it's perfectly legitimate to investigate him historically, and, in fact, that we ought to.

So join me in a quest to learn what we can about Jesus. You may be surprised at what you'll find.[1]

---

[1] All biblical quotations, unless otherwise noted, are from *The Holy Bible: English Standard Version* (Crossway Bibles, 2001).

1

Can We "Know" *Anything* about Jesus?

So Many "Jesuses"!

"To Tell the Truth" was a popular television game show in the 1960s and 70s. Three people appeared before a panel of celebrities, all claiming to be the same person, usually someone who had done something extraordinary (or, sometimes, just something weird). After several minutes of questioning, the panelists would vote for the person they believed was telling the truth. The climactic moment came when the host (Garry Moore) would say, "Will the real _____ please stand up?" Then the truth-teller would be revealed and the impostors exposed.

When you listen to the amazing variety of current descriptions and interpretations of who Jesus is, you might find yourself wanting to say with Garry Moore, "Will the real Jesus *please* stand up?"[1] Jesus is arguably the most significant person in human history and is still attracting all kinds of attention from scholars, religious devotees, and the entertainment world, but not all of it is helpful in understanding who he really is.

The group of scholars known as "The Jesus Seminar" describes him as a wandering Jewish story-teller who never said anything to offend or upset anybody.[2] Others portray him as a charismatic healer, a magician, a social reformer, or a political revolutionary,

[1] This very pertinent question became the title of a book on Jesus: Paul Copan, editor, *Will the Real Jesus Please Stand Up? A Debate between William Lane Craig and John Dominic Crossan* (Baker, 1998).

[2] This is because they conclude that Jesus actually said only about 18 percent of the words the Gospels attribute to him. It should be noted that they arrived at this conclusion by voting on each saying, and the conclusions were by no means unanimous.

to mention only a few. The 1970s musical "Godspell" pictured him as a dancing clown with no serious mission. "Jesus Christ Superstar," another musical adaptation of the Jesus story, presented him as a disillusioned celebrity who, by the time he reached Gethsemane, said, "Then I was inspired; Now I'm sad and tired." Mel Gibson's 2004 film "The Passion of the Christ" portrayed Jesus as a suffering martyr but offered no clear sense of his identity. More recently, Dan Brown's *The Da Vinci Code* and Michael Baigent's *The Jesus Papers* have popularized the idea that Jesus wasn't at all who the New Testament and Christians represent him to be, but was rather a non-divine man who became the subject of an elaborate cover-up designed to hide his real identity.

Even those who don't try to redefine Jesus have contributed to the confusion over his identity. Many devoutly religious people talk about Jesus constantly but tend to define him in terms of their emotions ("Jesus is the one who warms my heart and gives me peace."), without ever stopping to realize that he was a real person on the scene of human history and not just "a name for a feeling." These believers are often surprised (and sometimes disturbed) to learn there are many facts that can be known about Jesus.[3]

There's really nothing new about all of this. The great theologian Helmut Thielicke once wrote, "Over and over, the figure of Jesus has been horribly amputated to suit each age's taste." The eminent Yale historian Jaroslav Pelikan has observed that "the way any particular age has depicted Jesus is often a key to the genius of that age."[4] In other words, the variety of interpretations of who Jesus is may tell more about us than about Jesus. We are prone to define him as we want him to be, regardless of any known facts about him. As a result, everyone today is talking about "Jesus," but they mean radically different things from one another when they use his name.

---

[3] "Many Christians have been, frankly, sloppy in their thinking and talking about Jesus, and hence, sadly, in their praying and in their practice of discipleship. We cannot assume that by saying the word *Jesus*, still less the word *Christ*, we are automatically in touch with the real Jesus who walked and talked in first-century Palestine....": N. T. Wright, *The Challenge of Jesus: Rediscovering Who Jesus Was and Is* (IVP Academic, 1999), 10.

[4] Jaroslav Pelikan, *Jesus Through the Centuries: His Place in the History of Culture* (Harper & Row, 1987).

Our task is to find out what we can really know about Jesus. Not the Jesus of modern reconstructions or the Jesus of our emotions, but the Jesus who actually lived and died during the time of the First-Century Roman Empire.

Is It Possible to "Know"?

At this point some will undoubtedly hit their mental brakes and ask, "But can we really 'know' *anything* about Jesus?" And, "Isn't one interpretation of Jesus just as valid as another?" So I need to clarify the nature of our inquiry. We are asking, what can we know *from history* about Jesus? What kind of objective information is available to inform our understanding of him?

I fully realize in posing the question this way that some will doubt we can really know anything because they (perhaps you) believe there is no such thing as "objective reality," that reality is simply what the individual perceives it to be. So let me start from scratch in claiming we *can* know something about Jesus, that there is such a thing as "objective reality" about him, as well as about other things.

The objective view of reality—that there are some things that are universally true and knowable—has three primary characteristics:

(1) *Truth (reality) is what it is, regardless of the individual's perception of it.* In other words, what is true is true whether you or I think so or not. For example, on July 20, 1969, Neil Armstrong became the first man to walk on the moon, an event which the world celebrated as an astounding achievement of modern technology. Although most assume this event to be factual, there are many people who deny that it ever happened. As early as 1976, conspiracy theorists began to write books claiming the entire "event" was in fact an elaborate hoax, staged under top-secret conditions at the mysterious "Area 51" in the Nevada desert.[5]

---

[5]Bill Kaysing and Randy Reid, *We Never Went to the Moon: America's Thirty Billion Dollar Swindle* (Health Research, 1976). Two more recent claims of this nature include Charles T. Hawkins, *How America Faked the Moon Landings* (GTI, 2004), and Philippe Lheureux, *Moon Landings: Did NASA Lie?* (Carnot USA, 2003).

The conspiracy theorists claim it is scientifically impossible for anyone to walk on the moon, NASA in 1969 did not have adequate technology to land anyone on the moon, the photographs of the first moon walk betray signs of being obvious fakes, and even supposed "accidents," which took the lives of astronauts in subsequent years, were in fact assassinations to get rid of those who were threatening to expose the truth. There is an international organization of like-minded people who maintain that the moon-walking episode was an elaborate deception, cleverly orchestrated by the U.S. Government.

My point here is not to argue that Armstrong did or didn't walk on the moon. My point is that, if he did walk on it, it really doesn't matter what these people think or say; he still did it. If he didn't do it, it doesn't matter what the rest of us think; it never happened. That's objectivism.

(2) *Reality is supportable by evidence.* If something is objectively true, those who support it can produce evidence in its favor. This may be in the form of eyewitnesses, documents, or arguments concerning its reasonableness and/or probability. That doesn't mean the evidence is necessarily persuasive to everyone, but there will always be some evidence to back up the claim. In the case of Armstrong's moon-walk, there are film footage, documents, and the testimony of people who worked on the project. Naturally, the validity of their testimony has to be tested, but the very idea that it *can* be tested argues for an objective view of reality, doesn't it?

(3) *By implication, whatever contradicts reality is necessarily false.* Two opposite claims can't both be true, at least not when we're talking about events of history. If Armstrong walked on the moon, it is false to say he didn't. If he didn't, it's false to claim he did. It is simply impossible that he both did and he didn't.

What does all of this have to do with Jesus? Just this: either there was such a person or there wasn't. Either he was what the sources of evidence say he was, or he wasn't. Either he did what the sources say he did, or he didn't. So all of the conflicting views of Jesus can't be factual. There may be some overlapping factuality among some of them, but when they say opposite things about Jesus, one or more of them have to be in error.[6]

The Role of Historical Inquiry

In order to answer our question, "What Can We Know about Jesus?" we have to ask questions of a *historical* nature. We can't just offer up what we think or feel or have heard others say. We must ask about the evidence. That's why the objective view of reality is a requirement for serious historical work.

"But don't the sources of evidence need to be tested?" someone might ask. By all means! We want to test the evidence, and we are able in many instances to do so. But we must not retreat into a kind of agnosticism that refuses to see what the evidence really is and prefers instead just to say, "We can't know anything." That's intellectually dishonest and lazy.

Does the evidence always answer our questions specifically? Is there still room for disagreement? No one would claim that asking and seeking to answer historical questions about Jesus will tell us everything that we want to know, or answer every question we can ask and has been asked. Likewise, historical inquiry will never by itself be able to remove all our doubts or establish beyond question what actually happened or was said. Honest historical inquiry establishes *probability*. In other words, in seeking historical answers to our questions, we can only expect the evidence to point to what most *probably* happened. In the case of Jesus, people often ask, "Isn't it possible that Jesus went to India and studied Eastern mysticism?" "Isn't it possible that Jesus was married and had children?" In all honesty, from a strictly historical perspective, we can only answer, "Of course it's possible." But the real question is, is it *probable* that he did any of these things? Is there any *evidence* to indicate he did, other than simply someone's speculative notions or vivid imagination? It's the lack of historical perspective that is the cause of so many unfounded ideas about Jesus. That's

[6]For more on the objective view of reality, see Norman L. Geisler's chapter, "Why I Believe Truth Is Real and Knowable" in *Why I Am a Christian: Leading Thinkers Explain Why They Believe* Revised and Expanded Edition, eds. N. L. Geisler and P. K. Hoffman (Baker, 2006), 33–52.

what this book is about: encouraging you to think about Jesus from the perspective of history, rather than through the various lenses our culture presently offers or even through the lens of your own thoughts or feelings.

So What about Faith?

If you are a Christian believer, you may be wondering, "Where does *faith* come into this discussion?" That's a valid and important question. As a believer who has also wrestled with these questions, allow me to offer the following suggestions:

First, faith has nothing to fear from history. Going back to our discussion about objective reality, as believers we have to be concerned about what's true. I don't know about you, but I don't want to believe something false about Jesus just because it's attractive or comforting to me. If historical inquiry dispels some of my cherished notions, so be it. My faith will only be stronger and purer for being based on reality rather than illusion.

Second, a truly biblical faith is rooted in history. In the Old Testament, Israel established her identity as the people whom God had brought out of bondage in Egypt. What they believed was rooted in what had happened to them as a people. Likewise, the apostles preached Jesus as having lived, died, and risen from the dead in time and space—not simply as a "religious myth" and certainly not as a set of "holy emotions." Believers should want to know what happened and allow their faith to be informed and shaped by history.

Third, the Bible itself represents a blending of faith and history. The biblical authors don't just "tell what happened." They interpret what happened and reflect on its meaning for the lives of believers. We can expect the New Testament Gospels not just to tell us the story of what Jesus did, but to tell it in such a way that will compel us to follow him. After all, that's why they were written, as the Gospel of John frankly acknowledges (John 20.30–31). So in our inquiry about Jesus, it's perfectly okay to combine history and faith in the discussion. In fact, in one sense, it's impossible for them not to be. Even the most objective historian will tell the story of what happened in a way that attempts to shape our perception of it.

Fourth, the acceptance of any evidence is, to some extent, an act of faith. It simply means we trust the sources. For example, few of us (I hope) doubt that George Washington lived or that he was the first President of the United States. Why? After all, we never met him or even saw him. But, we have made either a conscious or unconscious decision to accept the sources (parents, teachers, textbooks, etc.) as accurate. That's what Christians (and sometimes others) do where the Bible is concerned. If we decide it's trustworthy, we're inclined to believe what it says about Jesus and allow it to answer for us some questions that cannot otherwise be answered. If we reject the Bible as a trustworthy source of information, then we'll be more skeptical and more open to accepting other views about who Jesus was and what he did. But remember, we need to ask those nagging questions about *probability*. As we'll see in the next chapter, the Bible is a valid historical source for our knowledge about Jesus.

So please accept this invitation to ask the basic questions that need to be answered in order to know anything for certain about Jesus. Whether you're a believer or not, stay with me and see where the evidence leads. And maybe you'll see the real Jesus stand up.

Additional Note: What Is the "Jesus Seminar"?

The Jesus Seminar is a group of approximately 200 scholars (mostly American) who take a very negative view of the historical reliability of the New Testament Gospels. Organized in 1985 by Prof. Robert Funk, the group began meeting in order to discuss various portions of the Gospel records in order to evaluate their authenticity. They used a highly controversial system of voting on each of Jesus' sayings by using an assortment of colored beads. Using this method, they concluded that Jesus spoke only approximately 18% of the words attributed to him in the Gospels. Their findings were published in 1993 in a book called *The Five Gospels: The Search for the Authentic Words of Jesus*. A later volume, *The Acts of Jesus: What Did Jesus Really Do?* reported similar negative conclusions regarding the deeds of Jesus as recorded in the Gospels.

While the Jesus Seminar never represented a "mainstream" of New Testament scholarship, as they liked to claim, they were more successful than most scholars in using the media to circulate their findings. Articles and programs on their conclusions were reported in most major newspapers, news magazines, and on television. As a result, they have had a tremendous impact on popular thinking about Jesus and the Gospels.

Among the criticisms leveled at the Jesus Seminar are the following:

- Their operating principle that the "Jesus of History" (i.e., Jesus as he really was) and the "Christ of Faith" (Jesus as Christians came to believe him to be) were not and could not be the same.

- Their insistence that the background for Jesus' words and deeds is to be found in ancient Hellenism rather than ancient Judaism, even though Jesus was clearly a First-Century Jew.

- Their rather loose historical methodology, as illustrated in the claim that the non-canonical "Gospel of Thomas" probably represents an earlier form of gospel writing than that found in the New Testament, even though "Thomas" cannot be dated any earlier than the Second Century AD.

- The use of the "criterion of dissimilarity" as a major factor in determining the authenticity of sayings attributed to Jesus. In other words, if something reportedly said by Jesus sounds like what ancient Judaism or the early church believed, then it must be disregarded as inauthentic. This leads to the odd conclusion that Jesus and his Jewish contemporaries, and even his own followers, could have agreed about very little.

- The conclusion that Jesus was not and never claimed to be Israel's Messiah, God's Son, etc., but was rather a wandering philosopher known for his kindness and story-telling. The reconstructed Jesus produced by the Seminar raises the question of how to account for his crucifixion, a fact attested to by ancient writers both in and outside the New Testament. Why would anyone want to kill such a man?

In other words, the Jesus Seminar had in mind from the beginning that Jesus was not who the Gospels claimed, and they developed a methodology that guaranteed they would affirm that conclusion. In spite of their claims, their efforts can hardly be considered to be objective scholarship.

Think About It

1. Why do you think there are so many different ideas about Jesus? Are these helpful in understanding who he was or not? Can you think of another figure in history who has been so variously interpreted?

2. Evaluate the often-heard statement: "It's impossible to know anything for sure." What does such an idea do to the effort to understand history?

3. Evaluate this statement: "Two opposite claims can't both be true." Can you think of any exceptions?

4. In making a historical inquiry, why isn't it enough to ask if a supposed event of the past is "possible"?

5. If faith has nothing to fear from history, why do you think people of faith have so often been opposed to historical inquiry about Jesus?

6. Explain this statement: "The Bible is a blending of faith and history." Why is this important in understanding the Bible?

7. In what way is the acceptance of evidence about anything an act of faith?

2

How Do We Know About Jesus?

If we're going to ask historical questions about Jesus, we have to find out what sources we have to work with and what kinds of information they furnish. Mostly, these sources are in the form of ancient writings that mention Jesus. In the interest of objectivity, we'll start with the non-Christian sources.

What Did Non-Christians Say About Jesus?

First, I should point out that we don't have a large number of non-Christian sources that tell us about Jesus. This may come as a surprise to many, since Jesus is so widely known today. How could it be that writers in and shortly after his own time overlooked him? The answer is that Jesus lived and died in relative obscurity and therefore was not even known to most of his contemporaries. He was born in a backwater of the Roman Empire to a poor Jewish family, and, as far as we can tell, he never traveled outside his very small homeland, except for the brief period when he was a baby and his parents took him to Egypt to escape Herod's murderous wrath (Matt 2.13–15). The events surrounding his death were regarded by those who knew about them as the results of a squabble among Jews, who were themselves looked down upon by their non-Jewish contemporaries. So it isn't really that surprising that more ancient writers didn't take notice of him. In fact, it might be more surprising that any of them did.

But, in fact, some did. And they fall into two categories: pagan (i.e., neither Christian nor Jewish) authors and Jewish authors. Let's start with the pagans.

Pagan Sources About Jesus

Tacitus was a Roman historian of the early Second Century AD. Around the year 115, he wrote the following comment regarding the great fire of Rome which occurred in AD 64 and was rumored to have been ordered by the emperor Nero himself:

> But all human efforts, all the lavish gifts of the emperor, and the propitiations of the gods, did not banish the sinister belief that the conflagration was the result of an order. Consequently, to get rid of the report, Nero fastened the guilt and inflicted the most exquisite tortures on a class hated for their abominations [*flagitia*], called Christians by the populace. Christus, from whom the name had its origin, suffered the extreme penalty during the reign of Tiberius at the hands of one of our procurators, Pontius Pilatus, and a most mischievous superstition, thus checked for the moment, again broke out not only in Judea, the first source of the evil, but even in Rome, where all things hideous and shameful from every part of the world find their center and become popular. Accordingly, an arrest was first made of all who pleaded guilty, then, upon their information, an immense multitude was convicted, not so much of the crime of firing the city, as of hatred against mankind. Mockery of every sort was added to their deaths. Covered with the skins of beasts, they were torn by dogs and perished, or were nailed to crosses, or were doomed to the flames and burnt, to serve as a nightly illumination, when daylight had expired. Nero had thrown open his gardens for the spectacle, and was exhibiting a show in the circus, while he mingled with the people in the dress of a charioteer or drove about in a chariot. Hence, even for criminals who deserved extreme and exemplary punishment, there arose a feeling of compassion; for it was not, as it seemed, for the public good, but to glut one man's cruelty, that they were being destroyed. (*Annals* 15.44.2–8).[1]

---

[1] J. Stevenson, *A New Eusebius* (London, 1957), 2–3; quoted in Everett Ferguson, *Backgrounds of Early Christianity* 3rd ed. (Eerdmans, 2003), 593. Both Stevenson and Ferguson can be consulted for the quotations which follow in this chapter. Also, these and many more quotations from ancient sources are available in *The New Testament Background: Writings from Ancient Greece and the Roman Empire That Illuminate Christian Origins* rev. edition, ed. C. K. Barrett (HarperSanFrancisco, 1995).

Notice, first of all, that Tacitus was certainly no fan of Christianity! So we can't accuse him of being biased in favor of Jesus or his followers. Also, he corroborates some information about Jesus given to us in the New Testament: that he was called "Christus" (Latin for "Christ"); that he was executed "during the reign of Tiberius" (see Luke 3.1); and that his executioner was none other than "Pontius Pilatus," the then-governor of Judea.

Suetonius was another Roman historian who lived in the late First and early Second Centuries. He doesn't say much about Jesus but does include this note concerning an edict (usually dated AD 49) issued by the emperor Claudius, who ruled AD 41–54: "Since the Jews constantly made disturbances at the instigation of Chrestus (Claudius) expelled them from Rome" (*Claudius* 25.4). The name "Chrestus" (from the Greek *chrestos*—"kind, loving") is apparently Suetonius' misunderstanding of Jesus' title "Christ" (Greek, *christos*—equivalent to Hebrew *mashiach*—"anointed one, messiah"). We can't be certain, but it seems likely that Suetonius is here referring to conflicts between Roman Jews and Jewish Christians, which he understands to have been instigated by "Chrestus" himself. (Remember, the Romans thought little of intra-Jewish squabbles, and even when they tried to find out what was going on, they often misunderstood them—see Acts 23.26–30; 25.13–22.) So although Suetonius doesn't tell us much, he does reveal that he was aware of Jesus, even if he had no clear idea who he actually was.

Another pagan source is even more interesting. In AD 112, Pliny, the Roman governor of the province of Bithynia, wrote a letter to the emperor Trajan, asking him how he should deal with people who were accused of being Christians. Should he ferret them out for prosecution, or deal with them only if they were brought before him and formally accused? (We are fortunate to have Trajan's reply, and he says that Pliny should take the latter course. At this point in history, Christianity was an illegal religion, largely because Christians refused to sacrifice to the image of the emperor.) Pliny's letter is rather lengthy, so I won't give the whole quotation, but one part is of extreme interest. Describing Christian worship meetings, he says,

That they were wont, on a stated day, to meet together before it was light, and to sing a hymn to Christ, as to a god, alternately; and to oblige themselves by a sacrament (oath), not to do anything that was ill: but that they would commit no theft, or pilfering, or adultery; that they would not break their promises, or deny what was deposited with them, when it was required back again; after which it was their custom to depart, and to meet again at a common but innocent meal, which they had left off upon that edict which I published at your command and wherein I had forbidden any such conventicles. (*Epistles* 10.96)

In addition to the fact that Pliny mentions "Christ" by name, it is noteworthy that he understands the Christians worshiped him "as … a god," even at this early date (an indication that the belief in Jesus' deity was not a late development as some argue), and saw their commitment to Christ as binding a highly moral life-style upon them. This isn't Pliny's only mention of "Christ"; elsewhere in the letter he says some "cursed Christ" when accused, in order to escape punishment.

Two pagan authors of lesser importance who wrote about Jesus are Celsus and Lucian of Samosata, neither of whom had much use for Jesus or Christianity. Celsus' work *True Discourse* (AD 177–178) is known to us from a quotation in the writings of Origen, a Third-Century Christian apologist. According to Origen, Celsus invented a conversation between a Jew and Jesus in which the Jew claims that Jesus was not virgin-born (as the Gospels of Matthew and Luke claim) but that Mary was an adulteress who was impregnated by a soldier named Panthera. This name is probably a play on the Greek word for "virgin" (*parthenos*). Celsus also claims that Jesus studied magic in Egypt, then returned to Palestine and proclaimed himself to be a god. Lucian, who lived around AD 115–200, says that Christians revered Jesus as a god and then makes a rather garbled reference to "the man who was crucified in Palestine because he introduced this new cult into the world" (*The Passing of Peregrinus* 11). It is unclear whether or not Lucian thought Jesus was that crucified man or not. While it is obvious that neither Celsus nor Lucian cared much for Christianity or for Jesus, they at least bear witness that he lived, that he was believed to have been born of a virgin, and that he was crucified.

So much for the pagans; now to the Jews.

Jewish Sources About Jesus

By far the most significant Jewish author is Josephus, a historian of the late First Century AD. Josephus wrote extensive accounts of Jewish history and, along with the New Testament itself, is our chief source of information about Judaism in the time of Jesus. In his 20-volume work called *Antiquities of the Jews*, published in AD 93–94, he said this regarding the high priest Ananus: "And so he convened the judges of the Sanhedrin and brought before them the brother of Jesus, the one called Christ, whose name was James, and certain others, and accusing them of having transgressed the law delivered them up to be stoned" (*Antiquities* 20.9.1). Notice that Josephus knows both Jesus' given name and also that he was "called Christ" (Messiah). He also confirms the New Testament information that Jesus had a brother named James (Matt 13.55; Gal 1.19).

A second reference to Jesus in the *Antiquities* is more controversial:

> Now there was about this time Jesus, a wise man, *if it be lawful to call him a man; for he was* a doer of wonderful works, a teacher of such men as receive the truth with pleasure. He drew over to him both many of the Jews and many of the Gentiles. *He was [the] Christ.* And when Pilate, at the suggestion of the principal men amongst us, had condemned him to the cross, those that loved him at the first did not forsake him; *for he appeared to them alive again the third day; as the divine prophets had foretold these and ten thousand other wonderful things concerning him.* And the tribe of Christians, so named from him, are not extinct at this day. (*Antiquities* 18.3.3)

What makes this passage controversial is the overt claim that Jesus was more than a man and that he was Israel's Messiah who was raised from the dead. The problem is, Josephus, not being a

Christian, probably didn't believe any of that. What we have here, in all likelihood, is a legitimate text from Josephus in which he mentions Jesus, but which has been re-worked by a Christian editor. Read the passage again leaving out the overtly Christian parts (which I have italicized), and you probably have the gist of what Josephus actually wrote. What is important, however, is that Josephus, even as a non-believer, confirms many things about Jesus that are also said in the Gospels: he was a teacher (Luke 18.18), he drew his followers from both Jews and Gentiles (John 12.20–21), he was executed by Pilate at the "suggestion" of Jewish leaders (Matt 27.1–2, etc.), he was crucified, and his followers were a distinctly recognizable group within Judaism and were called Christians (Acts 11.26; 1 Pet 4.16). That's lots of important information.

One other passage in Josephus is of interest in connection with Jesus. In *Antiquities* 18.5.2 he has a lengthy passage on John the Baptist, who he describes as a man who exhorted the Jews to lead righteous lives and who preached repentance and baptism. He also notes that John was feared by Herod Antipas (see Mark 6.19–20) because of his influence over the people, and that Antipas eventually had him imprisoned and executed. This rather accurately reflects what the New Testament says about John and his preaching, even though in this text Josephus does not mention John's connection with Jesus.

The other important Jewish source about Jesus is the collection of writings known as the Talmud, dating from the Fifth to Sixth Centuries AD, although many of the rulings and comments by the rabbis contained in it come from an earlier time, perhaps as much as a century or more. I won't cite any of them here, but there are numerous references to Jesus. Most of them acknowledge him to have been a miracle-worker, but the usual claim is that he was a sorcerer. None of the writings denies that he ever existed or that he worked miracles, even though the authors are highly antagonistic toward Christianity. While this might come as a surprise to modern Western readers, it should be remembered that in the ancient world there was a common belief in the reality of miracles, so it perhaps would not occur to the authors of the

Talmud to deny that Jesus could actually work miracles. It was more important to them to deny that God was the source of his power (see Mark 3.22).

So, what can we conclude concerning these pagan and Jewish sources about Jesus?

First, they confirm that he actually lived. In light of the evidence of Roman and Jewish historians, as well as others, to attempt to deny that Jesus existed is an exercise in historical blindness. One still hears the claim occasionally that Jesus never existed, or that we can't know from history that he existed. Those making these claims are either ignorant of the evidence or dishonest in ignoring it.

Second, they confirm several of the basic facts about Jesus which are stated in the Gospels. They establish that he lived in Palestine in the First Century AD, he had a brother named James, the Jewish leadership called for his death, he was crucified by the Romans during the governorship of Pilate, he was known as a teacher, his ministry was characterized by miracle-working, he was believed by his followers to have been the Messiah, he was worshiped as Deity, and his followers were called Christians. The non-Christian sources do not give us any additional information that was not already recorded in the Gospels, but their corroboration is of great importance, since it comes from sources that could hardly be accused of being biased in favor of Christianity.

How Important Are the Gospels?

Because the pagan and Jewish sources offer so little information about Jesus, we are left with the fact that the vast majority of what can be known about him comes from the New Testament Gospels of Matthew, Mark, Luke, and John. Each of these four authors presents a particular portrait of Jesus, which not only gives us information about who he was and what he did but also offers an interpretation of his importance and describes him in a variety of ways. That's why there are four, not one, and why they aren't all alike.

The Gospel of Matthew was written primarily for a Jewish audience, to present Jesus as the royal Messiah of Israel. Matthew opens his book with a 42-generation genealogy of Jesus, in order to prove his descent from David (since the Messiah was expected to be David's "son"—i.e., descendant). He also fills the Gospel with references to various Old Testament texts, which he shows to have been "fulfilled" by Jesus. There is also a sub-theme of Jesus as a sort of "new Moses," the great Lawgiver and Teacher of Israel. Matthew is composed of five major speeches (found in chs 5–7, 10, 13, 18, and 24–25), which are alternated with narrative (story) segments. These speeches contain most of Jesus' teachings in Matthew's Gospel. Many scholars see in them a symbolic representation of the "Five Books of Moses" (or Pentateuch—Genesis, Exodus, Leviticus, Numbers, Deuteronomy) with which the Old Testament opens. Also, just as Moses went up on Mt. Sinai to receive the Law from the hand of God, Jesus goes up on a mountain to deliver his Sermon on the Mount (Matt 5–7), which contains considerable material relating to the Law of Moses. All of this would have rung in with Matthew's Jewish readership.

Mark's Gospel, on the other hand, was apparently intended mostly for Gentiles. Unlike Matthew, when he uses Jewish terms or refers to Jewish customs, he always defines or explains them, assuming his readers won't know what he's talking about otherwise (see, for example, 7.1–4, 11). Because the Romans especially were impressed by power, Mark presents Jesus as the powerful, miracle-working Son of God. He calls him "Son of God" in the very first verse of his Gospel, and near the end of it the Roman in charge of the crucifixion says, "Surely this man was the Son of God!" Everything in between is designed to make this point. Whereas Matthew presents significant portions of Jesus' teaching, Mark focuses instead on his actions, recording seventeen miracles and only four parables. In keeping with this emphasis, Mark records numerous occasions on which Jesus cast out evil spirits; the first miracle he records in chapter 1 is of this type. To heighten the sense of action in his Gospel, Mark uses the word *euthus* more than forty times. It is often translated "immediately," but in some contexts this makes little sense, and so it is sometimes translated as "just then," "suddenly," etc. However it is translated, it is clearly an action word and highlights Mark's emphasis on Jesus as the doer of powerful deeds.

Luke is the only New Testament Gospel written by a Gentile (the only non-Jewish author in the New Testament). He writes to show that Jesus is "good news" (the meaning of the term "gospel") for all of humanity, both Jews and Gentiles, and especially for those on the fringes of society. To do this, he shows Jesus encountering and offering healing and salvation to those who were marginalized in Jewish society: the poor, lepers, tax collectors, women, and even Samaritans, the group perhaps most despised by his Jewish contemporaries. Luke is also the Gospel writer who takes the most pains to locate Jesus in a particular historical setting (although none of them ignores this aspect of his life). For example, his Prologue (1.1–4) suggests a writer who has done his homework by reading the accounts of Jesus written by others and by consulting those who were eyewitnesses (which he does not claim to be). And Luke 3.1–2 is a remarkable historical note, intended to pinpoint the time of John the Baptist's (and therefore Jesus') public appearance and ministry. In ancient terms, this is a very specific dating of Jesus' activity. Luke is the only Gospel writer to mention a Roman emperor by name. He also tells in some detail a portion of Jesus' life passed over by the other Gospels—the "travel narrative" (chs 9–19), which records Jesus' leaving Galilee and heading for Jerusalem for the final time in order to be crucified. Characteristically for Luke, this section shows Jesus continuing to focus attention in both his teachings and actions on those who were without power or status.

Matthew, Mark, and Luke are known collectively as the "Synoptic Gospels." They are called this because they follow the same basic outline in telling the story of Jesus, and the word "synoptic" comes from a combination of two Greek words which means "to see alike."

John's Gospel was written to present Jesus as the divine "Word" (Greek, *Logos*: John 1.1) of God, through whom alone God reveals his true nature and will. John doesn't tell us as much about Jesus' deeds as do the Synoptics (for example, he records no accounts of Jesus casting out demons) but offers much more of an interpretation of who Jesus was, primarily by means of speeches by Jesus himself. In contrast to the Synoptic Gospels, John is arranged more thematically than chronologically, so it's sometimes difficult to correlate his material with that found in Matthew, Mark, and Luke. But John is the most blatant about what he is up to -- to win over the reader—and he's the only one who addresses the reader directly with the second-person "you" in John 20.30–31: "Now Jesus did many other signs in the presence of the disciples, which are not written in this book; but these are written so that *you* may believe that Jesus is the Christ, the Son of God, and that by believing *you* may have life in his name."

Another distinctive feature of John is his openness about stating Jesus' identity and uniqueness. Unlike the Synoptics, in which Jesus seems determined to keep his identity as Messiah from being generally known, in John he openly states who he is (probably because in John most of the action is in and around Jerusalem where Jesus is in conflict with the leaders of Judaism; in the Synoptics most of the action is centered in Galilee, and Jesus didn't want to start a "messianic uprising" by people who misunderstood what he meant by the term "messiah").

It is important to realize that it isn't the purpose of the Gospels to offer a complete "life of Jesus," which is obvious when you notice what they omit about Jesus' life. In a modern biography, we would expect to find information about a notable person's early life, education, interests, etc. But most of what the Gospels tell us centers on the final three years of Jesus' life, with special attention given to the last week, especially his death and resurrection. The Gospels are sometimes described as "Passion Narratives with a long introduction" because of their heavy emphasis on the events of Jesus' final week. For example, these events occupy the last eight of Matthew's 28 chapters, the last six of Mark's 16 chapters, the last five and one-half of Luke's 24 chapters, and the entire second half of John (chs 12–21). It's obvious what the authors thought were the most important aspects of the Jesus story, isn't it? Only one of the Gospels, Luke, tells us anything at all about

Jesus as a child, and that is only one brief episode when he was twelve years old (Luke 2.41–52). Otherwise, the early life of Jesus (from about two years of age until about 30) is passed over in complete silence. They leave us with many unanswered questions about which we might be curious. But it isn't their intention simply to supply information or to satisfy our curiosity. Their goal is to tell us the most important things about Jesus: who he was and what he did and what he accomplished. And without them, we would know very little about him.

But Can We Trust Them?

Now we come back to the question of the credibility of our sources. This question arises in connection with the Gospels (and less so with Suetonius, Tacitus, etc.), because we are now talking about distinctly Christian literature. So, are the Gospels believable? Can they be trusted to give us accurate historical information about Jesus, or are they, as many claim, merely prejudiced religious documents of little historical worth?

This is a large and complex question, and I wouldn't try to make you think that I can adequately deal with it in these few pages. For a thorough treatment of this topic you should consult F. F. Bruce's classic *The New Testament Documents: Are They Reliable?* or Paul Barnett's more recent work, *Is the New Testament Reliable?*[2] Both of these are by world-class historians who can direct you to all the important points to be considered. I'll just hit the high points in this discussion.

We need to ask why so many people question the reliability of the Gospels in the first place. There are lots of reasons, but here are the main ones.

Some are bothered by the fact that the Gospels were written by Christians, so they conclude the authors obviously can't be objective when writing about Jesus. That may sound like a fair point, but let's look at it more closely. It certainly is *possible* that Matthew, Mark, Luke, and John have concocted or distorted a story they want to sell to their unsuspecting readers. But remember, we

---

[2]F. F. Bruce, *The New Testament Documents: Are They Reliable?* 6th ed. (Eerdmans, 1981); Paul Barnett, *Is the New Testament Reliable?* 2nd ed. (InterVarsity, 2005).

have to ask, not what is *possible*, but what is most *probable*. And it doesn't seem very probable that the Gospels are trying to fool us.

For one thing, if they were just making everything up, it's surprising that they included some of the things they did. Take the virgin birth story, for example (found only in Matt 1 and Luke 1). Although it has some significant differences with pagan mythologies about the gods cohabiting with human women, on the surface it gets awfully close, and the very idea of such a miraculous conception and birth is a stumbling block for many. So why would Matthew and Luke include it if they knew it wasn't true? Wouldn't they have been intelligent enough to realize that they were creating a problem that the church would have to deal with from then on? And what about Jesus' baptism by John the baptizer? John's baptism was "a baptism of repentance for the forgiveness of sins" (Mark 1.4). Yet Jesus came to him to be baptized and insisted on doing so, even over John's objection (Matt 3.14–15). But the New Testament consistently says that Jesus was sinless! (See, for example, 2 Cor 5.21; Heb 4.15; 1 Pet 2.22.) Why would the authors make up this story, since it raises a difficult question that is still discussed by scholars and theologians today? And why tell the story about Jesus becoming angry at what he saw in the Temple and driving out the animals and their sellers with a whip? And why include all of those embarrassing stories about the disciples' failures to believe who Jesus was, their squabbles among themselves, and their pettiness toward people who weren't part of their little group? That doesn't sound like a made-up story to me. Does it to you? And if the Gospels are so honest about these problematic and potentially embarrassing things, doesn't that argue for the probability that they would tell the truth in other areas as well?

Another reason some question the Gospels' accuracy has to do with the time-lapse between the events of Jesus' life and the time of the writing of the Gospels. Most scholars believe that, at the very earliest, the Gospels were probably written some 40 to 70 years after the time of Jesus (that is, AD 70–100), although some scholars would argue for dates as much as 30 years earlier. So, the argument goes, isn't it obvious there was quite a lot of "development" of the story during the interval, so that what we have is more of a mythological portrait of Jesus than a historically factual one?[3] Let me point out in reply that a standard is being applied here to the Gospels that is not applied to other writings from antiquity. No one that I am aware of questions the ancient histories of Julius Caesar and other notables, yet the documents telling their stories have at least as large a gap between the historical events and the recording of those events as what we have with the Gospels. Besides, we have a source even closer in time than the Gospels—the letters of the apostle Paul—and he confirms much of what is in the Gospels. Paul began writing his letters in the late 40s of the First Century, so he wrote about 20 years earlier than the earliest Gospel writer. And he confirms belief in Jesus' deity and in his death and resurrection. So if the story was embellished, it happened in much less than 40 years. That would mean there were still people alive who had seen and heard Jesus. If what Paul, Matthew, Mark, Luke, and John said wasn't true, they had a really tough sell.[4]

Besides, why must we assume that, because the Gospels were written by Christians, they can't possibly be telling the truth? That's a really odd assumption, when you stop and think about it. It's like saying that, in order to find out the facts about a historical event, you must talk to someone who wasn't involved and who has no real interest in the subject. If you wanted to learn what it was like at Omaha Beach on D-Day or in the World Trade Center on September 11, 2001, would you assume that you could only

---

[3]British New Testament scholar J. D. G. Dunn has recently argued that we must remember that the message about Jesus was originally an oral one, not contained in documents, and we should not assume that the oral tradition (as it is called) about Jesus is automatically less reliable than that of documents. This recognition somewhat closes the gap between the events themselves and their being written down, since it should be recognized that the written records were dependent on the oral tradition. J. D. G. Dunn, *A New Perspective on Jesus: What the Quest for the Historical Jesus Missed* (Baker Academic, 2005), 35–56, 79–125.

[4]For more on the question of the reliability of the Gospels, see Gary R. Habermas, "Why I Believe the New Testament is Historically Reliable," in *Why I Am a Christian: Leading Thinkers Explain Why They Believe* rev. and exp. edition, eds. N. L. Geisler and P. K. Hoffman (Baker, 2006), 161–174.

get the facts by talking to someone who *wasn't* there? Wouldn't it make sense to consult those who were eyewitnesses or who had talked with eyewitnesses? That's what we have in the Gospels.

"But aren't there discrepancies in the Gospel records themselves?" you might ask. That depends on what you mean by "discrepancies." Quite often two of the Gospels will record the words of Jesus differently, but that only shows they weren't slavishly copying one another's words to produce a verbatim account. (Wouldn't *that* raise suspicions if they all agreed in every detail?) Rather, they each give the sense of what Jesus said, sometimes re-worded to make a specific point, but not in a contradictory way. (See Matt 3.17 and Mark 1.11 for an example, where Matthew has apparently re-worded the message of the "voice from heaven" in order to direct it to the reader rather than to Jesus himself.)

Granted, there are some historical questions raised in the Gospels that aren't easily explained. For instance, Luke says Jesus was born in Bethlehem rather than in his parents' hometown of Nazareth because of a census in the days when Quirinius was governor of Syria (Luke 2.2). But according to Josephus (*Antiquities* 18.1), Quirinius served as governor at a later time (AD 6–9) and ordered a census at that time. It would be strange for so careful a historian as Luke to make such a blunder, so some suggest that perhaps Quirinius served as governor of Syria at an earlier time also, but the evidence for this is inconclusive. Likewise, the Synoptic Gospels say that Jesus' Last Supper with his disciples was a Passover meal and that he was crucified the next day (Mark 14.12; Luke 22.15). However, the Gospel of John seems to indicate he was crucified on "Preparation Day," just prior to the Passover (John 19.31). There are several possible explanations for this, but no one can be sure what the real explanation is. But such "discrepancies" (which may have perfectly valid explanations that are simply beyond our historical information) in no way affect the message of the Gospels about who Jesus is and what he did. The very fact that someone might raise these as objections to the Gospels' credibility shows there isn't that much to say against them.

The objections to the Gospels' reliability operate on an assumption that, when you really think about it, seems quite unfair and unrealistic. That is the assumption that the early Christians were aware that all (or much) of the Jesus story was made up but bought into it anyway and then tried to convince their friends and neighbors of its truthfulness. Or they didn't know the difference and had been hoodwinked by the apostles and other leaders. Why do we assume that they were either so naive or so dishonest? That really doesn't square with what we know of them otherwise (remember Pliny's statement about their morality?). And remember, the apostles (with the exception of John) were all executed for their preaching of a Jesus who was God's Son, crucified, and risen from the dead. Yet, according to the skeptics, they knew it was a lie. How probable is *that?*

In looking for reasons why some are so skeptical about the Gospels, one thing has to be acknowledged: Some people simply have a pre-determined bias against anything supernatural or miraculous. They've already concluded that nothing like that can be true, so when they read about Jesus' being the divine Son of God and working miracles, their minds automatically assume it can't be true and they start looking for alternative explanations. I mention this only to caution that the accusation of bias cuts both ways. Many who assume that the Gospels can't be true because the authors were Christians are predisposed to disbelieve them simply because they themselves are not.

Don't Forget the Rest of the New Testament

We've talked about the four Gospels of the New Testament first because they are of first importance in gaining information about Jesus. But we shouldn't overlook the fact that the rest of the New Testament contains important information about him, too.

Especially important are the letters of Paul. The New Testament contains 13 letters that are attributed to Paul (although the authenticity of some of them—2 Thessalonians, Ephesians, Colossians, 1 and 2 Timothy, Titus—is questioned by some scholars). These letters date from approximately AD 48–49 until around AD 65. As noted above, based on the usual dating of the Gospels (generally AD 70–100), that means that all of Paul's letters may have been written before any of the Gospels were. That being the case, they constitute an earlier source of information about Jesus than even the Gospels themselves. (Remember that our New Testament is arranged in logical—not chronological—order. The Gospels come first, not because they are the earliest written portions of the New Testament, but because the story contained in them is assumed in all the rest of the New Testament documents.)

The problem is, however, that, due to the nature of his letters as teaching and "trouble-shooting" documents, Paul doesn't tell us a great deal about the *story* of Jesus. He assumes that his readers already know the story. But what he does say is important, because it shows what was generally known and believed about Jesus among Christians around the middle of the First Century and within 20 to 30 years of Jesus' own life. Some historians maintain that Paul actually didn't know much about Jesus' life. One British historian, G. A. Wells, has gone so far as to maintain that Paul is "silent" about Jesus' life.[5] While it is obviously true that Paul doesn't fill his letters with references to the facts and events of Jesus' life or with quotations from his sayings, it is far from true that he is either ignorant of or silent about them. For example, Paul mentions that Jesus was descended from Abraham (Gal 3.16); that he was a "son" (i.e., descendant) of David (Rom 1.3); that he was "born of a woman" and lived under the Jewish law (Gal 4.4); that he welcomed all kinds of people (Rom 15.5–7); that he lived a life of humility and service (Phil 2.7–8); that he was abused and insulted (Rom 15.3); that he had a brother named James, as well as other brothers (Gal 1.19; 1 Cor 9.5); that he was betrayed and instituted the Lord's Supper on the night of his betrayal (1 Cor 11.2, 23–25); that he appeared before Pilate (1 Tim 6.13); that the Jews of Judea participated in his death (1 Thess 2.14–15); and that he was buried, rose on the third day, and made numerous appearances following his resurrection (1 Cor 15.4–8). It should be not-

---

[5] G. A. Wells, "Earliest Christianity," *The New Humanist*, Vol. 114, No. 3, (Sept. 1999): 13–18. See also Wells' *The Jesus Myth* (Open Court, 1998) and *The Jesus Legend* (Open Court, 1996).

ed that these details are conveyed incidentally—that is, Paul isn't deliberately trying to re-tell the story of Jesus. This implies that he knew more than he told, but he saw no need to write more. Also, all of these details are (later) confirmed by the Gospels, without any exaggeration or distortion.

In addition to demonstrating knowledge of Jesus' life, Paul also is obviously informed about many, if not all, of Jesus' teachings. We've already mentioned his references to Jesus' words at the Last Supper (1 Cor 11.23–25/Matt 26.26- 29). In addition, Paul knows Jesus' thoughts on divorce and remarriage (1 Cor 7.10–11/ Mark 10.2–12); quotes his teaching that the laborer deserves his wages (1 Cor 9.14/Matt 10.10); repeats Jesus' views that all foods are clean (1 Cor 10.27/Mark 7.18–20); bases his own teaching about paying taxes on what Jesus had said on the same subject (Rom 13.7/Luke 20.25); draws on Jesus' imagery of his eventual return as being like that of a "thief in the night" and entirely un-predictable (1 Thess 5.2–5/Matt 24.36–44); and echoes many of Jesus' ethical teachings from the Sermon on the Mount (Rom 12.9–13.10/Matt 5.43- 7.12).

So to suggest that Paul didn't know much about Jesus is to ac-knowledge that one doesn't know much about Paul. It should also be noted that most of the references to Paul's writings cited above come from letters whose authenticity is *not* disputed by anyone. Obviously, Paul does not add to our fund of information about Jesus, since what he says is also said in the Gospels, but he con-firms that what is said in those later writings was already common knowledge among Christians.

It is sometimes asked, "How did Paul know about Jesus?" Af-ter all, he wasn't one of the 12 who traveled with Jesus and knew him first-hand (at least, we have no evidence of any first-hand contact, though such is not historically impossible since Jesus and Paul were contemporaries). There are three possible sources for Paul's information. First, Paul says in Galatians 1.18–19 that he had some first-hand contact with those who were eyewit-nesses of Jesus, particularly Peter and James the brother of Jesus. Certainly one of their major topics of discussion on such an occasion would have concerned things Jesus did and said. (Can you imagine them *not* talking about these things?) Second, it is generally acknowledged that prior to the writing of the Gospels, stories and sayings of Jesus were circulated by word-of-mouth (this is called "oral tradition"). It seems likely that one of the first things every new convert was taught was as much of this tradition as his or her teachers knew; Paul would have been no exception. Third, Paul himself claims to have received his gospel message by divine revelation and not through human interme- diaries (Gal 1.11–12, 16; 1 Cor 11.23; 15.3). This doesn't mean he learned everything that way, nor does it rule out the first two sources of his information listed above; it only suggests that he regarded the core of his message as having come directly from God himself. But even if one discounts the probability of divine revelation, Paul had ample opportunity to learn the things he said about Jesus.

While Paul is the most important New Testament source for information about Jesus (other than the Gospels), since he is the earliest to write, the other New Testament writers such as Peter, John, and James, as well as Luke in the book of Acts, are likewise important witnesses to Jesus. Peter, John, and James were all in first-hand contact with Jesus. Acts describes approximately the first 30 years of the movement Jesus began (the appearance of which must somehow be accounted for historically), and the book of Revelation presents Jesus as the Lord of history and even of eternity. While each of these writings is unique, they all testify to the reality of the man known as Jesus of Nazareth.

Other Sources?

Are there any other Christian sources about Jesus outside the New Testament itself? Yes, but they don't help us much, partly because they are so much later in origin and partly because they contain obviously mythological elements. (Read them, and you'll understand why Matthew, Mark, Luke, and John got into the New Testament and these others didn't.) One category is called "Apocryphal Gospels," documents about Jesus which were written in the Second through Fourth Centuries AD. These contain mostly supposed "sayings" of Jesus (many of which are probably authentic, although not recorded in the New Testament) and very little narrative (story). And some were obviously intended to promote speculative views about Jesus. These are the "Other Gospels" and "Lost Gospels" you see touted in the bookstores as if they were something new and exciting. They aren't new, and most aren't all that exciting either, although some are more interesting than others.

Perhaps the best-known of these gospels is the "Gospel of Thomas," probably dating from about the middle of the Second Century AD. It is a collection of 114 supposed sayings of Jesus. Some of them parallel or are adaptations of sayings found in the New Testament Gospels, but others are clearly of Gnostic origin or at least are sympathetic with Gnostic views of Jesus. (The Gnostics were a heretical group who made a distinction between the man Jesus and the divine Christ and who were a serious thorn in the side of more orthodox believers by the Second Century.) The "Gospel of Thomas" has gained a lot of attention in recent years, mostly because of the claim by members of the Jesus Seminar that it represents a type of "original gospel" that supposedly pre-dates the New Testament Gospels. This an odd claim, since by all estimates "Thomas" dates well after Matthew, Mark, Luke, and John. And one would wonder how much interest there would have been in a collection of Jesus' sayings if there had not been written accounts of his life previously, since "Thomas" contains no story of Jesus at all.[6]

Falling into another category of "other gospels," the "Infancy Gospel of Thomas" (not to be confused with the "Gospel of Thomas") is one of several works which were written to try to fill in the gaps in our knowledge about Jesus' life prior to age 30.

---

[6]For a full discussion of the "Gospel of Thomas" and other apocryphal gospels and how they are often misused by critics, see Chapters 3 ("Questionable Texts—Part I") and 4 ("Questionable Texts—Part II") in Craig A. Evans, *Fabricating Jesus: How Modern Scholars Distort the Gospels* (IVP, 2006). From a slightly different angle, see the helpful summary in Ben Witherington III, *What Have They Done With Jesus?* (HarperCollins, 2007), 27–48.

Remember that only Matthew and Luke record Jesus' birth, and only Luke records an episode from his childhood. We are told nothing else about Jesus until he was baptized by John, when he was "about 30" years old (Luke 3.23). That leaves lots of interesting questions unanswered, doesn't it? What was the Son of God like when he was eight? Since he had brothers and sisters, how did he get along with them? Did he know who and what he was? What was he like as a teenager? Did he have divine powers? Did he use them? The "Infancy Gospel of Thomas" seeks to answer some of those questions, but not in a very convincing way. It basically portrays Jesus as a divine brat who uses his powers to punish anyone who displeases him (even striking some of his playmates dead!). He's a highly precocious boy who makes clay birds fly and stretches a piece of wood when his father, Joseph, cuts it too short. Again, compare such things with what you find in the New Testament Gospels, and the Gospels only look better.

So why didn't the "Apocryphal Gospels" make it into the New Testament, and were they "suppressed by the church," as critics often claim? To answer the first question, the Apocryphal Gospels didn't make it into the New Testament because they really aren't gospels at all. They contain very little of the story of Jesus, and none of them describes Jesus' death and resurrection from the dead—the "good news" which gives the term "Gospel" its meaning. Second, these "gospels" weren't so much "suppressed" as dismissed as being of little value. Almost all of them have the goal of redefining Jesus according to Gnostic views, and in the process contradict what was commonly known about Jesus in Christian circles. As the eminent New Testament scholar Bruce Metzger once wrote, "Even a casual acquaintance... of these gospels and their credentials will convince the reader that no one excluded them from the Bible; they excluded themselves."[7]

---

[7]Bruce M. Metzger, *The New Testament: Its Background, Growth, and Content*, 3rd ed. (Abingdon, 2003), 122. For a recent evaluation of the apocryphal gospels and their significance, see Darrell L. Bock, *The Missing Gospels: Unearthing the Truth Behind Alternative Christianities* (Nelson, 2006).

The Bottom Line...

So we're left with this historical fact: Our chief sources of information about Jesus are the four Gospels found in the New Testament. If we can't trust them, then we can know very, very little about Jesus at all. If they are trustworthy, which seems most probable, then we can know quite a lot, though not as much as we might like. The other sources are useful, but mostly because they confirm that Jesus lived and because they confirm the essential outline of the story found in the Gospels. Even the rest of the New Testament doesn't add a great deal to our data about Jesus, but it shows that other ancient writers, some of whom wrote earlier than the Gospels, believed and taught the same things.

I hope this is helping you understand how it's possible to know about Jesus, mostly because we have a four-fold record in the New Testament. And it's really quite a compelling record. But don't just take my word for it. Read it for yourself.

Additional Note 1: Was Jesus an "Exorcist"?

Although it is commonplace to refer to Jesus as an "exorcist" and to his casting out of demons as "exorcisms," the New Testament suggests that this isn't quite accurate.

"Exorcism" means the casting out of a spirit through the use of ritual. Exorcism rituals vary from religion to religion but usually include the recitation of prayers, sacred words or formulas, and sometimes the use of sacred objects. Some exorcists even employ the infliction of pain on the theory that, if the body becomes uncomfortable enough, the demon will be driven out!

But the Gospels portray Jesus as simply "casting out" the demons by the power of his word. "With authority he commands even the unclean spirits, and they obey him" (Mark 1.27). The usual term used for Jesus' activity in casting out evil spirits is the Greek word *ekballo*, which simply means "to throw out." You might say Jesus "evicted" the demons by the power of his word.

To refer to Jesus as an "exorcist" seems to miss an important point the Gospel writers make: that he was not like the exorcists with whom their readers were already familiar (see Acts 19.13–16, the only time the word "exorcist" is used in the New Testament). Rather than having to rely upon secondary power sources, he had the authority within himself to command the spirit world, and his onlookers found this amazing.

Additional Note 2: BC/AD or BCE/CE?

It has long been customary to mark ancient time references by the use of the abbreviations BC. ("Before Christ") and AD (Latin for Anno Domini, "in the year of our Lord"). However, out of deference to non-Christians who might resent the implied faith-confession of these references, many authors have abandoned the traditional designations in favor of BCE ("Before the Common Era") and CE ("Common Era"). However, in this study I have retained the use of BC and AD for the following reasons:

1. Regardless of whether one uses BC/AD or BCE/CE, time is still being dated from Jesus' birth (approximately at least; our calendars are slightly miscalculated, and Jesus was most likely born no later than 4 BC).

2. Since this book is written from a Christian perspective, it only seems appropriate to use the customary Christian designations. They are part of our overall view of history and the impact of Jesus upon it.

3. Both Judaism and Islam, as well as other religions, have their own calendars which, of course, are not dated around Jesus' birth. No one would deny them the right to use their own methods of marking the centuries in their writings, nor should anyone be offended at their doing so. So, Christians should feel no compulsion to abandon the BC/AD designation in ours.

Additional Note 3: Judas Wrote a Gospel?

When "The Gospel of Judas" was released in April, 2006, some scholars declared that it would revolutionize our understanding of Jesus and the nature of early Christianity. Especially, we were told, it would completely reverse our understanding of the relationship between Jesus and Judas Iscariot, the disciple who is typically referred to in the New Testament as "the one who betrayed him." Why? Because "The Gospel of Judas" says Jesus actually *asked* Judas to betray him and suggests that Judas was Jesus' closest disciple to whom he revealed the innermost secrets of the kingdom.

But "The Gospel of Judas" wasn't really all that drastic a revelation—and it wasn't written by Judas, in spite of its name. The manuscript of "Judas" was discovered in the 1970s and dates from approximately AD 300. However, an early Christian writer named Irenaeus mentions a work by that name in his five-volume treatise *Against Heresies*, written about 180. Assuming this is the same document and that the writing of it was 25–30 years previous to that (long enough to become known), "Judas" probably dates from about AD 150—much too late to have been written by Judas Iscariot.

So what about the claim that Judas betrayed Jesus by request? The key to this comes near the end of the document, when Jesus says, "You will sacrifice the man that clothes me." You see, "Judas" is one example of the well-known category of "Gnostic Gospels," sometimes referred to as "apocryphal gospels." The Gnostics were an off-shoot of Christianity who believed that matter is evil and spirit is good, a concept drawn from Hellenistic philosophy. This dualistic world-view made it impossible for Gnostics to accept such a doctrine as the Incarnation of Jesus, that is, that he was a pre-existent being who "became flesh" (John 1.14). From the Gnostic point of view, there's simply no way that a divine being—let alone God himself—could actually become flesh. So some Gnostics claimed the Christ-spirit merely inhabited the body of a man named Jesus, but they were actually separate beings. That meant, for example, that when Jesus died on the cross, the Christ didn't—he only *appeared* to do so. This form of Gnosticism is often called *Docetism*, from a Greek word meaning "to appear" or "to seem to be."

Therefore when Jesus says to Judas, "You will sacrifice the man that clothes me," this is simply another way of stating the Gnostic belief about Jesus. Like the other Gnostic Gospels, the purpose of "Judas" is primarily to (1) redefine Jesus according to the Gnostic understanding of his nature, and (2) set forth supposed "secret teachings," which were the stock-in-trade of the Gnostics (literally, "knowing ones," from the Greek word *gnosis*, "knowledge").

So Judas didn't write a gospel; someone wrote it in his name, just as other Gnostic gospels were written in the names of other apostles. And, as interesting as it is, it hasn't revised our understanding of either Jesus and early Christianity or Jesus' relationship with Judas, the betrayer.

Think About It

1. Explain why there aren't more non-Christian sources of information about Jesus from the ancient world. Does this surprise you?

2. Which do you think constitutes a more reliable source about someone from the past: an opponent or an admirer? Why?

3. What kinds of information do we gain from the non-Christian sources about Jesus?

4. Why are the New Testament Gospels of such singular importance in knowing about Jesus?

5. Why do you think that none of the Gospels offers us a complete "Life of Jesus"? How would our understanding of him be different if we had one?

6. List and evaluate some of the reasons why many people are skeptical of the Gospels' accuracy. Which do you think have the most validity? Which do you think have the least validity?

3

When, Where, and How Did Jesus Live?

The story of Jesus in the Gospels doesn't begin, "Once upon a time, there was a man named Jesus," although that is the way many people seem to think of him, rather than as someone who actually lived in time and space.

Well, that isn't what the Gospels say. Listen to Luke's impressive emphasis on the historical setting of Jesus' life and ministry:

> In the fifteenth year of the reign of Tiberius Caesar, Pontius Pilate being governor of Judea, and Herod being tetrarch of Galilee, and his brother Philip tetrarch of the region of Ituraea and Trachonitis, and Lysanias tetrarch of Abilene, in the high priesthood of Annas and Caiaphas, the word of God came to John the son of Zechariah in the wilderness. (Luke 3.1–2)

Luke tells us who was emperor of Rome, who was governor of Judea, who were the tetrarchs ("rulers of a fourth part") of the various parts of Palestine, and who were the reigning and immediate past high priests of the Jews at the time John and Jesus began their public ministries. Likewise, Matthew says Jesus was born in Bethlehem of Judea "in the days of Herod the king" (Matt 2.1). All of the rulers listed above by Matthew and Luke are well known to historians from sources outside the New Testament, and their dates can be reasonably fixed by existing information. It quickly becomes clear that the Gospel writers want to locate the life of Jesus in a specific time and place in history. But when was that time, and where was that place?

So When Was It?

In spite of the great time distance between us and Jesus, we can fix some of the dates of his life with reasonable certainty, as long as we don't insist on hitting the *exact* years. (This, by the way, is how it is with all ancient history, not just the story of Jesus.) Let's start with his birth.

Matthew 2.1 says Jesus was born "in the days of Herod the king" (mentioned also in Luke 1.5). Although Rome was firmly in control of Palestine all during the time of Jesus and for several centuries after, they permitted the Jews to have their own "puppet kings," rulers who were hand-picked by Rome and whose number-one job description was to watch out for the interests of the Empire. The New Testament writers refer to several of these kings as "Herod." It turns out that there are five "Herods" mentioned in the New Testament, since "Herod" was a dynastic title rather than just a personal name. (The other four are Herod Antipas [Matt 14.1] who beheaded John the Baptist; Antipas' brother, Philip, whose wife Antipas had married, leading to John's beheading [Mark 6.17]; Herod Agrippa I [Acts 12] who killed James the apostle; and Herod Agrippa II [Acts 26] who heard Paul's defense.)

The Herod mentioned as reigning at the time of Jesus' birth is the one known as "Herod the Great." We know a great deal about him (largely from Josephus), and he was an interesting character in his own right. He was a brutal, superstitious tyrant who killed anyone and everyone that he suspected of posing a threat to his power. This is evidenced by the episode of the "Slaughter of the Innocents" recorded in Matthew 2.16–18, an event not confirmed by non-biblical writers, but entirely consistent with what we know of Herod's character. So why was he called "the Great"? Because he was a very capable administrator who got along well with the Romans (too well, many of his Jewish contemporaries thought) and who completed a number of impressive building projects. The most significant of these was the complete renovation and expansion of the Temple in Jerusalem, which he turned into a spectacular complex of buildings and adjacent structures. (This project was begun, but not nearly completed, during his reign.)

So how does all of this help us date the birth of Jesus? Well, our friend Josephus tells us that Herod the Great reigned from 37 BC to 4 BC, and the New Testament tells us that Jesus was born during his reign. If the "BC" ("Before Christ") part catches your attention, then you're way ahead of me. Yes, that's right: Jesus was born "BC"! The problem is, there is a glitch in our calendars. They are supposed to be calculated from the time of Jesus' birth, but "Dennis the Small" (the monk who devised our calendar) made a slight miscalculation which, when corrected, puts Jesus' birth sometime during or prior to 4 BC, while Herod the Great was still living and reigning.

If you look closely at Matthew 2.16–20 again (when Herod killed all those children in Bethlehem, hoping to destroy Jesus), it seems that Jesus may have been as old as two years at the time. Herod was probably hedging his bets by killing "all the male children in Bethlehem and in all that region who were two years old or under, according to the time that he had ascertained from the wise men." But he had made some pretty careful calculations about this, so we can safely conclude that Jesus could possibly have been as old as two, but was probably a bit younger. Putting all of this together, most scholars calculate Jesus' birth somewhere in the range of 7–5 BC.

Our next touch-point for dating Jesus' life is the beginning of his public ministry. And here we have some direct help from one of the Gospels. Luke 3.23 says that Jesus was "about thirty years of age" when he began his ministry. Note that Luke's statement isn't as specific as we might like (was he 28? 30? 32?), but is very helpful nonetheless. Apparently, from what the Gospels tell us, Jesus lived in relative obscurity up until the time he appeared as a candidate for baptism by his relative, John the Baptist. Remember that Luke 3.1–2 places John's activity in the "fifteenth year of Tiberius Caesar," which would have been around AD 27–28. This squares nicely with what we have previously established—that Jesus was born 7–5 BC and was "about thirty" when he began his public ministry (about the same time that John began his).

But we can go even further by calculating the approximate

length of Jesus' ministry. Since his public ministry ended with his death, then we will know about when he died and his approximate age, if we can establish the length of his ministry with any reasonable certainty. And we can.

We do this by noting the number of times the Gospels record that Jesus went to Jerusalem for the Passover celebration, one of the most important feast days of the Jewish year. The Synoptic Gospels (Matthew, Mark, and Luke) each mention Jesus' attending only one Passover in Jerusalem—the one during which he was crucified. If we were limited to them, then, we might conclude that Jesus' public ministry (i.e., the time from his baptism and wilderness temptations until his death) lasted only one year or perhaps even less. However, the Gospel of John suggests a ministry of two to three years, since it mentions Jesus going to Jerusalem for Passover on three separate occasions (John 2.13; 6.4; 11.55). This could cover a period of as little as two or as many as three years (or a bit more). If the public ministry began in AD 27–28, as we concluded earlier, then Jesus died around AD 30, give or take a couple of years. This meshes very well with our secular (that is, not from the Bible) sources and their information about Jesus and the movement he began.

So in answer to the question "When did Jesus live?" we can safely answer that he was born around 7–5 BC, began his public ministry about AD 27–28, and died around AD 30. Pretty close calculations for something that took place almost two millennia ago.

And Where Was It?

This one's really easy, and no one seriously questions it. The New Testament gives ample evidence (as do the other sources) that Jesus lived and died in the land known as Palestine.

This area has a long and rich, though often tragic, history. It was the Promised Land which God had told the people of Israel that he would give to them, even before they were called the people of Israel. After their escape from Egyptian bondage, he led them in the wilderness for 40 years (because of their unbelief—they could have been there 40 years earlier; see Num 13–14). Finally, they were able to cross the Jordan into the Promised Land.

At the time it was known as "Canaan" and its inhabitants were the "Canaanites." But once the Israelites occupied it, it became known as "Israel." Later, the Romans designated it as "Palestine," and even today it is known by both of these latter names.[1] Palestine was and is a very small country. In Jesus' day it was about the size of the state of Maryland. After the Israelites' occupation of it, it had an interesting, if not always glorious, history. Located between Mesopotamia (where the kingdoms of Assyria, Babylon, and Persia were) and Egypt, Palestine was a strategic area in spite of its small size. Military campaigns between the great powers made control of Palestine of great importance. So it was often a "buffer state" between powers far greater than itself. It had enjoyed a measure of power and political independence during the reigns of its first three kings (Saul, David, and Solomon), but was much weaker after that. Still, control of it was of strategic importance, and it was almost always under the domination of some foreign power.

In the time of Jesus the dominating foreign power was Rome, which had taken possession of Palestine in 63 BC and continued to control it throughout the entire era of the New Testament and beyond. So, the Assyrians, Babylonians, Persians, Greeks, and Romans successively had control of this unhappy land. The statement by some Jews in John 8.33, "We are offspring of Abraham, and have never been enslaved to anyone," can only be taken as a symptom of nationalistic pride at the expense of history. In reality, they had been in bondage to just about everyone. And even as they spoke, they were not a free people. The Romans were firmly in control. They had permitted the Herods to rule as "puppet kings," and the Herods themselves were not pure-blooded Jews, but Edomites, the descendants of Esau, the twin brother of Jacob (whose other name was "Israel"). The Edomites were despised by the Jews. So the state of Judaism in Palestine when Jesus was born was one of great turmoil politically and spiritually. This was the world into which Jesus was born and in which he died.

---

[1]See both the helpful discussion and the maps in Tim Dowley, *Kregel Bible Atlas* (Kregel, 2002).

But we can be even more precise about Jesus' place of birth. Both Matthew and Luke place the event in the town of Bethlehem, a small village about five miles south of Jerusalem (Matt 2.1; Luke 2.1–7). But Jesus was known as "the Galilean," and Galilee is in the far northern part of Palestine. So why was he born in Bethlehem in the south? Luke explains why. It was because of the census that required every head of household to report to his ancestral home, not only to be counted but also to be taxed. So Jesus' parents, Mary and Joseph, made the long trek from their home in Galilean Nazareth to the "little town of Bethlehem," now immortalized in the Christmas hymn. Joseph was "of the house and line of David" according to Luke, so he had to report to "the city of David," Bethlehem. Naturally, he couldn't leave behind his pregnant wife, so the two of them had to make the arduous journey, and there Jesus was born. The exact movements of Joseph and his little family are not clear. Luke 2.39 simply reports that following Jesus' dedication at the Temple in Jerusalem, which would have occurred when he was 40 days old (Lev 12.1–6), "they returned into Galilee, to their own city." However, Matthew 2.13–23 says that at some point after Jesus' birth, Joseph was warned in a dream to flee to Egypt to prevent Herod from killing the infant king, and that through a series of divine interventions they eventually returned to their home city of Nazareth. Very likely this "flight into Egypt," as it is usually called, took place later than the events of Luke 2. Regardless of the exact timing of these things, Jesus grew up in Nazareth, his home town (Luke 4.16).

Jesus and His Family
Fortunately, we know a great deal about Jesus' ancestry, since both Matthew 1 and Luke 3 supply us with rather detailed genealogies. Such genealogies were very important in Jewish society as a way of establishing one's legal and spiritual heritage, and there are lots of them in the Old Testament. Jesus' genealogy was so important to Matthew, in fact, that he actually opens his Gospel with it. This makes for some tough reading for the uninitiated, but for a First-Century Jew, the roll call of names

from the Old Testament leading up to Jesus would have been like photos in a family album, with each name recalling some aspect of the long history of the Jewish people.

Although the genealogies in Matthew and Luke overlap for the most part, they are not at all identical. For one thing, Matthew begins with Abraham, the "father of the Jewish people," and works forward to Jesus. Luke, on the other hand, starts with Jesus and works backward all the way to Adam and even to God himself. The reason for this difference is that each writer had a different purpose in mind for his genealogy. Matthew wanted to show Jesus as a true Israelite and descendant of King David, fully qualified to be Israel's Messiah. Luke offers a more "universal" genealogy, one that shows Jesus' identification not just with Judaism, but with all humanity. There are a few instances in which the discrepancies in names between the two ancestor lists can't be reconciled, although numerous suggestions have been made. But this does not alter the fact that the Gospels give us a firmly-established sense of Jesus' place in Jewish history generally and of his family identity more specifically. So we know Jesus was from the tribe of Judah and descended not only from some of Israel's most illustrious persons, but also from some notorious rascals.

The presence of Joseph in both of Jesus' New Testament genealogies raises an interesting and often-asked question: If Jesus was born of a virgin, how can these genealogies be at all legitimate? Being virgin-born would mean that Joseph was *not* Jesus' "birth father," a fact acknowledged by both Matthew and Luke. For example, Luke's genealogy says, "Jesus… being the son (as was supposed) of Joseph…" (Luke 3.23). So why bother with the genealogies? One reason this is an important question is that the genealogies establish Jesus' ancestral qualification to be called "Messiah." If the genealogies aren't legitimate, then the Gospels' case is severely weakened. The answer is rather simple: In ancient Judaism, even an adopted son was considered to be the legal heir of his father's ancestry—and that is what Matthew in particular wants to establish: not that Jesus was physically descended from all of these people whom he lists, but that he is legally qualified to be

Messiah, since he is a legal descendant of David. (For an example of this, see Deut 25.5–6.) Look at it this way: If this were not the case, why would Matthew bother to give a genealogy at all, since it would do nothing to prove his point about Jesus' Messiahship?

We don't know much about Joseph and Mary, except that they were apparently an ordinary Jewish couple, aside from their notable son. Joseph was a tradesman, a carpenter (Matt 13.55). Jesus likely learned that trade as well (Mark 6.3), and is known even today as "the Carpenter of Nazareth." Not much is said about Joseph in the birth accounts (more in Matthew than in Luke; he isn't even mentioned in Mark), and he does not figure at all in Jesus' story afterward. Because of this, it has been assumed that he was probably dead by the time Jesus reached adulthood, although this cannot be verified. (Mary was apparently a widow by the time of Jesus' death, however, since John tells how Jesus made provision for his mother's care just before he died—John 19.26–27.) It was customary for Jewish men to marry women (girls, actually) much younger than themselves, so Mary's early widowhood is not at all unlikely.

Because of the Virgin Birth stories in Matthew and Luke ("virginal conception" is the more accurate term, since the conception, not the birth, is claimed as the miracle), Mary is naturally a much more interesting figure than is Joseph. We usually picture her at the time of Jesus' birth as a mature young woman, about the same age as her husband. However, Jewish girls were normally "betrothed" and then married between the ages of 12 and 14. This puts quite a different spin on our reading of Gabriel's appearance and announcement to her, doesn't it? Imagine an unmarried girl not more than 14 years old being told first that she will become pregnant, then that her baby will be the Son of God. It is an obvious testimony to Mary's piety and faithfulness that she responds, "Behold, I am the handmaid of the Lord; let it be to me according to your word" (Luke 1.38). After Jesus' birth Mary appears only infrequently in the story, and no miraculous powers are credited to her, nor is she assigned an on-going function in Christian faith and worship. While she is certainly presented as an admirable character (though by no means perfect—see Mark 3.21, 31–35), the New Testament never portrays her as anything other than a devoted (if not always understanding) mother.

As for Mary and Joseph's (and therefore Jesus') economic status, we can only say they were lower-class Jewish folk, the kind who would have been disdainfully called "the people of the land" by the more religiously-intense Pharisees and Sadducees who wielded the power and influence in Jewish society. How do we know this? One clue is given in Luke 2.22–24, which tells of Jesus' being taken to the Temple while still a baby. The Law of Moses required that, for the birth of a first-born male, his parents should sacrifice a lamb. But provision was made for the substitution of "two turtledoves or two young pigeons" for those who could not afford a lamb (Lev 12.6–8). Luke indicates that the poorer offering was made for Jesus, so we can readily conclude that Joseph and Mary were on the lower end of the socio-economic scale in Palestine. However, we should not conclude, as has often been done, that they were destitute. After all, Joseph was a tradesman, and there is no reason to believe he could not have made an adequate living for his family.

Speaking of Mary and Joseph's family, we should at this point say something about Jesus' brothers and sisters. Yes, the New Testament indicates that Jesus was not an only child, but that he grew up in a household full of children. Although some, in order to safeguard Mary's "perpetual virginity," maintain that Jesus had no siblings, the evidence says otherwise. For example, all four of the Gospels mention that Jesus had brothers (Mark 3.31–35; Matt 12.46–50; Luke 8.19–20; John 7.1–10), and Matthew and Mark even name them: James, Joseph, Simon, and Judas. John clearly states, and Matthew and Mark strongly imply, that Jesus' brothers did not believe in him during his time on earth. Both Matthew and Mark state that Jesus had sisters (Matt 13.56; Mark 6.3), but none of their names are given. Although this might surprise us in 21st-Century America, it was typical in ancient Judaism, as the Old Testament genealogies amply demonstrate. And in addition to the New Testament evidence, remember Josephus' statement that Jesus had a brother named James, who is mentioned because he had been brought before the Jewish authorities. While some might suggest that Jesus' brothers and sisters were actually his "cousins," or that they were step-siblings due to Joseph's earlier marriage to another woman (something for which there is no historical evidence whatsoever), these are merely attempts to salvage a theological viewpoint that is unsupported by the evidence we have. The indications are that Mary and Joseph had a house full of children (at least seven, if we assume at least two sisters), which would have been more typical of a First-Century Jewish household than would a single-child family. Again, the evidence makes sense.

Perhaps more would be said in the New Testament about Jesus' family, but he himself downplayed the importance of being related to him by physical birth. Once when a crowd was gathered about the door of the house where Jesus was staying, some reported to him that his mother and brothers were outside asking for him. "Who are my mother and my brothers?" Jesus asked. "And looking around at those who sat about him, he said, 'Here are my mother and my brothers! Whoever does the will of God is my brother, and sister, and mother'" (Mark 3.31–35). Partly as a result of these words, we are told very little about Jesus' relatives. Scholars widely believe, for example, that the New Testament letter of James was authored by Jesus' brother of that name. But the author identifies himself simply as "James, a servant of God and of the Lord Jesus Christ" (Jas 1.1). Perhaps he had learned well the lesson that it is spiritual relationship to Jesus that truly matters, not physical.

Jesus' Lifestyle

It has become fashionable in recent years to describe Jesus as "homeless," since he once said that "the Son of Man has nowhere to lay his head" (Matt 8.20), and because the Gospels describe him as moving about Galilee and making forays into the southern reaches of Judea as well. However, there are other indications that he may, in fact, have had a house which served as "home base" for him when he was not traveling about. Mark 3.20 says that at one point Jesus "went home," and the next verse indicates that this was not the home of either his parents or of his brothers and sisters. Later, Mark twice (7.17; 9.28) mentions "the house." It may be that these are simply references to various places where Jesus stayed rather than all referring to one location; nevertheless, it indicates that Jesus did customarily have a roof over his head.

A recent—and quite opposite—development in thinking about Jesus is the claim of some advocates of the "health and wealth gospel" (those who claim that God wants everybody to be rich) that he was a wealthy man, which is unfortunately used to try to justify believers' also striving to become rich. Supposedly, since Jesus had received the expensive gifts of gold, frankincense, and myrrh at the time of his birth (Matt 2.11), and since he had sufficient means to care for a large band of travelers who went about with him, he must have been a wealthy man. While there is nothing to suggest that Jesus was destitute, there is certainly nothing pointing to wealth. In fact, his teachings make this highly unlikely (Matt 8.20; Luke 12.13–21; 16.19–31; etc.) and certainly offer no comfort to those who would major in riches today. Besides, Luke says, not that Jesus provided for the apostolic group out of his own means, but that there was a group of women who traveled with him and the apostles and who "provided for them out of their means" (Luke 8.1–3).

The mention of the women and the group who traveled with Jesus raises the question of Jesus and his friends. Although making it clear that Jesus had many enemies, the Gospels also indicate that he had some very meaningful friendships as well. First, there were the 12 apostles who spent the better part of three years in his company, traveling with him and learning from him. Acts 1.15–26 indicates there were other men with them also, since two are put forward as potential replacements for Judas because they had been with Jesus from the time of his baptism until his ascension back into heaven—that is, throughout his entire public ministry. So, adding in the women mentioned in Luke 8, there were an indeterminate number of people who traveled about with Jesus at different times. Luke 10.1 mentions a group of 72 (or, according to some manuscripts, 70) who Jesus sent out to go ahead of him to the towns and villages. Of course, this doesn't mean that all of these were his close friends, but it does widen the circle of possibilities for those who might be called friends of Jesus.

Luke 10.38–42 records a visit by Jesus to the home of two sisters named Mary and Martha. We later learn from John 11 that these sisters also had a brother named Lazarus, and that Jesus "loved" both him and his two sisters (John 11.3, 5, 36). So there were evidently some people other than the disciples with whom Jesus became very close. We have no way of knowing how many others there may have been, but it is not surprising that someone so appealing as Jesus must have been would have had many friends, especially since he went out of his way to befriend many of those who were the most despised in Jewish society (Luke 15.1–2; 19.1–10).

Language, Education, Travels?

So, with the exception of its remarkable beginning and the final three years, we have every indication that Jesus' life was very ordinary. This is probably why the Gospels say nothing about it between the ages of about two and about 30 (with the exception of that one episode when he was 12) simply because it was, in most respects, the life of an ordinary Jewish young man.

So as an otherwise ordinary First-Century Jew, what language(s) would Jesus have spoken? Without question he spoke Aramaic, the Hebrew dialect that was the common language of Palestine. Significant on this point is the fact that the Gospels record Jesus' use of some Aramaic words, such as *abba*, his characteristic way of addressing God as "Father" (Mark 14.36), and his cry from the cross: *Eli, Eli, lama sabachthani*—"My God, My God, why have you forsaken me?" But since he grew up in Galilee, an area that was heavily influenced by Hellenistic culture, and almost within sight of the Greek-styled city of Sepphoris, he very likely spoke *Koine* (that is, "common," as opposed to classical) Greek as well.[2] The persistence of Greek as the trans-national

---

[2]Evans points out that the Greek influence in Sepphoris was much less pronounced prior to AD 70 than it was later, but acknowledges that many Galilean Jews spoke some Greek. See Craig A. Evans, *Fabricating Jesus* (InterVarsity Press, 2006), 113–122.

language of commerce and correspondence all around the Mediterranean basin is a testimony to the thoroughness with which Alexander the Great had Hellenized (imposed Greek culture on) the area three centuries earlier. Since Palestine was occupied by the Romans, there is likewise the possibility that Jesus knew, or at least understood, some Latin. The interrogation of Jesus by Pilate raises the question of which language they used. Of course, it is possible that they spoke through a translator. Even if Jesus did not speak fluent Latin, it is not improbable that Pilate spoke Aramaic, but there is no way to be sure of this. So we may safely conclude that Aramaic would have been Jesus' "heart language" and that he probably knew Greek and possibly Latin as well.

As for Jesus' education, the New Testament records nothing about his receiving any formal training. He probably was educated at home, as was typical in most Jewish families, and would also have received some instruction at the local synagogue in Nazareth (at which Luke 4.16 indicates he was a regular attendee). Some Jewish families employed tutors for their children, but, given that Joseph was a tradesman, it is unlikely that he could afford such a luxury. (The "Infancy Gospel of Thomas" records that Joseph did hire a tutor for his precocious son, who ended up striking the poor professor dead for presuming that he could teach him anything.) Luke 2.41–52 records Jesus' conversation in the temple with the teachers of the Law when he was only 12 years old and adds that "all who heard him were amazed at his understanding and his answers" (v 47). However, Luke does not attribute this to education and probably intends for the reader to understand that it came to Jesus naturally as the Son of God. But following this episode, Luke relates that Jesus "went down with them [Mary and Joseph] and came to Nazareth and was submissive to them" (v 51), suggesting that he completed his childhood under quite normal circumstances. Even with so little information available to us about Jesus' education, it is hardly likely, as some have begun to claim, that he was illiterate, especially since Luke records that he read aloud in the synagogue at Nazareth (4.16–20).

Back to the question of whether or not Jesus ever left Palestine and traveled to places such as India: With the exception of his brief sojourn in Egypt as an infant, which was noted earlier, we simply have no evidence that this was the case, and no sources contemporary with him indicate such a thing.[3] Likewise, we have nothing historical to the effect that he was ever married or had children (*The Da Vinci Code* notwithstanding). These are typical of the kinds of stories that were and continue to be invented about Jesus. But our concern is with history, not speculation or myth. And it seems, from a historical point of view, that none of these things happened.

It's amazing that someone from so ordinary a background, who lived in such common surroundings and never traveled outside his own country, would even be remembered today, much less be the focus of so much attention. Jesus both lived and died in Palestine, spending most of his life as an ordinary (though he was evidently anything but ordinary) Jewish peasant during the time of the Roman Empire, and suffering death by crucifixion at about the age of 33. Not a long life by most standards, but a very significant one. How significant? Well, we're still talking about him today, aren't we?

Think About It

1. List some of the historical touch-points for establishing the chronology of Jesus' life. Does it surprise you that we can date his birth, death, etc. as accurately as we can, or that we can't date them even more precisely?

2. Why was Palestine in such political and religious turmoil when Jesus arrived on the scene? How did this affect the nature of his life and ministry?

3. Does the realization that Jesus grew up in a fairly typical First-

---

[3]Unfortunately, this doesn't keep people from trying to manufacture numerous travels for Jesus. For a recent example, see William W. Mountcastle, *The Secret Ministry of Jesus: Pioneer Prophet of Interfaith Dialogue* (University Press of America, 2007), who claims on the basis of historically questionable sources that Jesus had a secret ministry in India, Tibet, and China.

Century Jewish family change your thinking about him in any way? If so, how?

4. Why is it helpful to know the languages that were important in Palestine in Jesus' day?

5. Why do you suppose that so many theories have been proposed about Jesus' travels outside Palestine and about his being married, when there is no historical evidence to support any of them?

4

How Jewish Was Jesus?

Throughout the history of Jesus studies, numerous theories and methodologies have been proposed that have in some instances advanced our understanding of Jesus—and in others have seriously retarded it. The "criterion of dissimilarity" definitely falls into the latter category. The criterion of dissimilarity was one of several criteria established by scholars who sought to recover the "authentic" words of Jesus, as opposed to those they believed were only attributed to him in the Gospels. This approach is based on the assumption that the "Jesus of History" (the Jesus who really was) and the "Christ of Faith" (what Christians came to believe about him) cannot possibly be the same person. So there must be some way to sort out the authentic from the invented in determining what "the real Jesus" actually said.

Central to this pursuit was the use of the criterion of dissimilarity: Anything that seemed to be in close agreement with the beliefs of the earliest Christians could not be regarded as authentically from Jesus, nor could anything that could be traced to the Judaism of Jesus' day. In other words, only that which was dissimilar from early Christian beliefs and those of First-Century Judaism could be considered as authentic. The idea was that if a saying of Jesus was too close (a very subjective judgment, as you can imagine) to either early Christianity or Second-Temple Judaism, then it obviously came from those sources rather than from Jesus himself. Naturally, this led to a very truncated notion of what Jesus actually said.

Amazingly, for several decades of the 20th Century, this criterion was widely accepted by scholars. Now, however, it is generally recognized as an extremely biased oversimplification that is bound to lead to an inaccurate portrait of who Jesus was and what he did and didn't say. It was logically flawed from the beginning, because it assumed that (1) Jesus and the early Christians didn't agree about much of anything and (2) that somehow Jesus managed to escape the influence of the Judaism in which he grew up and of which he was a part. Although the inconsistency of this view is now obvious to most, it continues to be employed by some, such as the members of the Jesus Seminar, who claim that Jesus must be interpreted against the background of Hellenism (Greek culture) rather than Judaism. Odd, since Jesus was a Jew who, as far as we know, never left Palestine during his entire adult life.[1]

Rather than expecting Jesus to differ radically from his Jewish contemporaries, we would expect him to be heavily influenced by Judaism and to reflect this in his own teachings and practices. Likewise, we would expect the Gospels' comments about him to reflect this Jewishness. And, in fact, that is exactly what we do find in the Gospels: Jesus is portrayed in the context of the Judaism of his own time, as a practicing Jew, but also as one who definitely put his own slant on things.

So we need to ask, "Just how Jewish was Jesus?" To what extent and in what ways did he reflect his Jewish heritage, and to what extent and in what ways did he depart from it? We can't possibly expect to have a clear historical picture of Jesus until we get some sort of answer to these questions. Fortunately, the Gospels offer us plenty of information to go on, as do other contemporary sources such as Josephus.

Jesus' Jewish Faith

Before proceeding further, it might be helpful to point out some of the indications that Jesus was, in fact, a devout practicing Jew who held strongly to the basic beliefs of Judaism in general, even though not without modifications.

---

[1]For a critique of the criterion of dissimilarity and of other criteria that are based on it, see James D. G. Dunn, *A New Perspective on Jesus: What the Quest for the Historical Jesus Missed* (Baker Academic, 2005), 58–69.

For one thing, it is evident from even a cursory reading of the Gospels that Jesus regarded the events recorded in the Hebrew Scriptures as factual. He made frequent reference to Old Testament teachings and events and to the lives of various characters recorded there in a manner that suggests full acceptance of their reality and validity (see, for example, Matt 11.20–24; 12.1–8; Mark 10.17–22; 12.24–27; etc.). Along with this, Jesus displayed a profound respect for the Scriptures themselves, as evidenced by the way he cited them. (See Luke 4.1–13, where Jesus responded to Satan's temptations by saying, "It is written…," followed by quotations from Deuteronomy.) In the Sermon on the Mount he declared his intention to fulfill, not abolish, the law and the prophets, declared that everything written in them must be accomplished, and warned against relaxing even the least of the commandments (Matt 5.17–19). Luke 4.16 records Jesus' attendance at the synagogue in his hometown of Nazareth, where he participated in the service by giving the reading from the prophets.

That same episode in Luke 4 says, "as was his custom, he went to the synagogue on the Sabbath day," indicating that Jesus was a habitual synagogue attendee. Matthew 17.24–27 indicates that Jesus paid the customary half-shekel tax which was collected for the support of the temple. Furthermore, Jesus adhered to the requirements of the Law by going to the temple during the Passover season and participating in the Passover meal with his disciples. There are even indications that Jesus acknowledged many of the Jewish institutions of his day, though not fully agreeing with them (Matt 23.1–3).

So there can be little question that Jesus was a devout practicing Jew. Still, we need to ask more specifically where Jesus fits into contemporary Judaism.

Judaism in Jesus' Day: Common Religious Emphases

First, it will be necessary to give at least a thumbnail sketch of what Judaism was like when Jesus walked the earth. We will do this by discussing what Jews generally believed alike, then by distinguishing among the various groups within Judaism and the ways they differed from one another.

What were the common characteristics of Judaism in the First Century AD? What did Jews generally believe alike that made them Jews and set them apart from other peoples in the ancient world?

Monotheism. This term simply means the belief that there is only one God. The Jewish people were alone among ancient peoples in believing in one God rather than in a pantheon of deities who controlled various parts of the universe and who were often in conflict with one another. (There was one brief period of monotheistic religion enforced by one of the Pharaohs in Egypt, but it lived only as long as he did.) This uniquely Jewish perspective is expressed in the verses known as the *Shema:* "Hear, O Israel: The Lord our God, the Lord is one. You shall love the Lord your God with all your heart and with all your soul and with all your might" (Deut 6.4–5). This cornerstone creed was recited twice daily by devout Jews and reflected the first of the Ten Commandments: "You shall have no other gods before (besides) me" (Exod 20.3; Deut 5.7). Isaiah 40–55 contains the classic prophetic critique of polytheistic idolatry, which the prophet mocks by describing a man who cuts down a tree, uses half of it for firewood to cook his dinner, and makes the other half into a "god" which he worships.

What makes the monotheism of the Jewish people all the more remarkable is the fact that the prevailing way of accounting for the gods of others in the ancient world was simply to adopt them as one's own—a practice known as syncretism. Enforced syncretism was one of the common methods of subduing conquered peoples, and the Jews had throughout their history been conquered by many foreign powers. But in general, they resisted this tendency, although they at times fell prey to it, as the prophets attest (Jer 2.4–13; Ezek 8.7–18; 1 Kgs 18.1–46; etc.). But the prophetic condemnation of it is evidence of their strong monotheistic beliefs.

Election. Based on God's covenant with Abraham (Gen 12 and 15), the Jewish people saw themselves as a uniquely chosen people through whom God would work to bring evil to an end. Their history was the history of God's redemptive acts in his world. This conviction inevitably led to a sense of exclusiveness which included a fear of racial (and thus religious) mingling. This concern became heightened during and just after the exile in Babylon, when remaining a people apart became a matter not just of theology but of survival. The Old Testament books of Ezra and Nehemiah show how this conviction operated in very practical matters in the period after the exile.

In the Gospels, this strong sense of election and its corresponding exclusiveness is evident in the conflicts between Jews and Samaritans. The origins of the Samaritans are not entirely clear, but they apparently sprang from the intermarriage of Jews who were left behind in Palestine during the exile with their Gentile neighbors. Once the Jews who had been exiled returned, having survived through strictly maintaining their Jewish identity in a foreign land, they were appalled that those who had been left behind had so readily compromised it. The result was centuries of hostility, mistrust, and rejection. The Samaritans, finding themselves excluded from the rebuilt Jerusalem Temple, withdrew from Judaism proper and established their own rival sanctuary on Mt. Gerizim in the northern part of Palestine ("Samaria"). This fact lies behind the discussion between Jesus and the Samaritan woman at the well in John 4. It also gives punch to Jesus' parable of the Good Samaritan: the very idea that a member of a despised race could possibly do the right thing, when a Jewish priest and a Levite had declined to do so.

The existence of the Jew-Samaritan conflict amply attests how important was the Jewish sense of calling and election as the exclusive people of God.

The Law. Going all the way back to the Exodus from Egypt and the giving of the Ten Commandments, the Law played a central role in Jewish belief and daily life. But after the destruction of the Temple by the Babylonians in 586 BC, the Law became something of a national preoccupation. There were two reasons for this. First, the Law was portable. With their Temple destroyed and having no priesthood to minister to them in a foreign land, they still had the Law to provide stability and guidance. Second, strict observance of the Law set the Jews apart from others, thus ensuring their survival no matter where they were. This was especially true of the laws concerning circumcision, clean and unclean foods, and the proper observance of the Sabbath day, since these practices were largely peculiar to Judaism.

The heightened focus on the Law during and after the exile probably accounts for the rise of the institution known as the synagogue. Although never mentioned in the Old Testament, the synagogue was an accepted part of Jewish religious and communal life by the time of Jesus. Synagogues apparently arose as places of prayer, study of the Law, and worship when the Jews were exiled away from their homeland. But they eventually spread even into Palestine, since for a time there was no Temple. They came to be dominated by the class of teachers known as rabbis, who were acknowledged experts in the Law.

The Temple. The Temple in Jerusalem was the focal point of the Jewish sacrificial system and of the annual observance of the various festivals required by the Law. The priesthood functioned in the Temple, overseeing the sacrifices. It therefore had a central importance to all Jews. It is important to distinguish between the Temple and the synagogues. There was only one Temple (except for that competing one acknowledged only by the Samaritans), and there the sacrifices were offered by the priests who were in charge. On the other hand, there were many synagogues, administered by synagogue rulers and teachers of the Law (not priests), and no sacrifices were offered there.

In spite of—and to some extent because of—its central importance to virtually all Jews, the Temple was also the focal point of sharp controversies within Judaism. During the Roman period, the Romans appointed the high priests to ensure cooperation with the conquering authorities. These leaders were often poorly qualified, if at all, and were frequently involved in political intrigue and gross violations of the standards of Jewish law. As a result, some Jewish groups, such as the Essenes, renounced the Temple and its priesthood as hopelessly corrupt and refused to have anything to do with it.

The Age to Come. After centuries of foreign domination, the

Jews of First-Century Palestine looked forward to a time when God would act to overthrow their oppressors and restore the nation to its former glory and independence, as in the days of David and Solomon. For many (although not all), this "golden age" would be inaugurated by a special leader known as the Messiah ("Anointed One"). Among those who believed in a coming Messiah, there were numerous ideas as to his identity, but most expected a warrior-king, a kind of "second David," who would overthrow Roman rule and restore Israel to prominence. Regardless of their messianic views, most Jews looked forward to "the restoration of Israel" (also known as "the consolation of Israel"—Luke 2.25—and "the coming of the kingdom"), a time of glory and independence.

Personal Piety. In addition to the prescribed sacrifices at the temple and the great public festivals and synagogue worship, Jews had common ways of expressing their personal devotion to God. These revolved around three principal acts of piety: the giving of "alms" (giving to the poor), prayer, and fasting. In the Sermon on the Mount, Jesus singled out these three acts to emphasize that one's devotion to God ought not to be done for show (Matt 6.1–18).

So these are some of the major beliefs and practices which Jews held in common in the time of Jesus. Keeping them in mind, let's look at ways in which they also differed among themselves.

Judaism in Jesus' Day: Diversity and Conflicts

At one time it was common to hear people say something like, "In the time of Jesus all Jews believed...." You don't hear that much anymore, because our knowledge of First-Century Judaism has expanded enough that we know it was too diverse for such statements to have much validity. True, as we have just seen, there were some basics on which most Jews agreed, but even in these areas they often differed significantly and sharply with one another. As a result, Judaism in the time of Jesus was not a monolithic entity; rather, it was characterized by wide diversity, as evidenced by the existence of several identifiable groups, each with its own peculiar slant on things.

Pharisees. The Pharisees are the Jewish group the Gospels mention most frequently, mostly because they are frequently found to be in opposition to Jesus over such matters as Sabbath regulations and purity laws. As a result, we get a generally (though not exclusively) negative picture of them.

Josephus says that there were about 6,000 Pharisees, and that they were very influential with the common people. Mostly they were made up of middle-class trades people. Their primary focus was on keeping the Law. In order to protect the Law, they practiced what they called "fencing" or "putting a hedge" around the Law.

This involved making rules that were even stricter than the Law itself—the idea being that if you don't cross the "fence," you won't trespass on the Law itself. The Pharisees had a very broad definition of what constituted "the Law," one with which not all of their contemporaries agreed. For the Pharisees the Law included not only the written Law of Moses found in the Old Testament, but also their "oral traditions" (sometimes called "the traditions of the elders"). These were the added rules mentioned above, which they believed went all the way back to Moses even if not written by him. Furthermore, their concept of the law was always expanding as new interpretations and applications of it were added to what was already written. Some of their distinctive beliefs (according to the New Testament) included the resurrection of the dead, life after death, and the existence of angels and demons (Acts 23.8).

Sadducees. The other primary group within First-Century Judaism, the Sadducees were from the upper classes. From this group came the priests who ministered in the Temple. So, whereas the Pharisees were more popular with the common folk, the Sadducees had control of the Temple and what went on there. Unlike the Pharisees, who steadfastly resisted Hellenistic influences, the Sadducees were more open to compromise, which also left them open to suspicion in the eyes of the average Jew.

Theologically speaking, the Sadducees had a much more restrictive view of the Law than did the Pharisees. They accepted as fully authoritative only the Torah ("instruction"—the books of Genesis, Exodus, Leviticus, Numbers, and Deuteronomy). Other

books of the Hebrew Bible had a lesser authority, and they rejected entirely the oral tradition of the Pharisees. They also rejected
the Pharisees' belief in an afterlife, angels, and demons. This is
reflected in the question posed by some Sadducees to Jesus during
the final week of his life concerning a woman who had been married consecutively to seven brothers: "In the resurrection, therefore, whose wife will the woman be?" Their point was that, since
this question could not be answered (or so they thought), there
must not be a resurrection (see Luke 20.27–40).

Essenes. As mentioned earlier, some Jews regarded the Temple
and its priesthood as hopelessly corrupt and so withdrew from
mainstream Jewish life, at least as far as it was oriented around
the Temple. The Essenes were one such group. Most of them
(there is evidence of an "Essene Quarter" in Jerusalem in the
time of Jesus) lived communally at Qumran on the shore of the
Dead Sea. They are thought to be the source of the Dead Sea
Scrolls, which give much insight into their beliefs and practices. The Dead Scrolls include copies of all of the Old Testament
books (except Esther), Essene commentaries on these books, and
documents pertaining to the specific thinking and regulations of
the Essene community.

The Essenes are not mentioned by name in the New Testament,
although Josephus does describe them. One possible allusion to
them may be found in Matthew 5.43, where Jesus says, "You have
heard that it was said, 'You shall love your neighbor and hate your
enemy'." Nothing in the Old Testament ever says to "hate your
enemy," and we have no knowledge of that being the teaching of
other Jewish groups. But it was an Essene teaching, and so Jesus
may be making a sideward reference to them.

The Essenes were apparently a relatively small communal sect,
but they are important because they remind us of just how diverse
First-Century Judaism really was.

Zealots. Because of the Roman occupation, there were (not
surprisingly) ardent Jewish nationalists who would do almost
anything to overthrow them. These nationalists were known as
Zealots, and their primary goal was the "restoration of Israel" to

political independence. Some were willing to resort to revolution and assassination in order to further this goal.

There is some question as to whether or not the Zealots were actually a separate group within Judaism or if there might not have been "zealous ones" among the Pharisees. One reason for this question is that Paul in two of his letters describes himself as having been "extremely zealous... for the traditions of my fathers" (Gal 1.14) and "as to zeal, a persecutor of the church" (Phil 3.6). However, it should be noted that in neither text does Paul speak specifically of *political* zealotry, although that may be included in "the traditions of my fathers." But the evidence for Paul as a Zealot is very slight.

What is certain, however, is that one of Jesus' own disciples is described as "Simon the Zealot" (Luke 6.15), suggesting he might at one time have been a rebel leader or at least politically involved in the Zealot movement. This is all the more intriguing when we recall that another of Jesus' disciples was Matthew (Levi) the tax collector—precisely the kind of Jew who might have been the target of a Zealot assassination.

Herodians. As their name implies, these were prominent (and presumably wealthy) Jews who supported the Rome-friendly policies of the Jewish puppet kings. Two New Testament references to them are particularly interesting. Mark 3.6 says they sided with the Pharisees in order to get rid of Jesus. Herodians and Pharisees would not normally, to the best of our knowledge, have sided with each other about much of anything. That they did so in this instance suggests the intense dislike that both groups had for Jesus. Likewise, Matthew 22.15–16 says that it was Herodians who tried to trap Jesus with a question about the validity of paying taxes to Caesar. This would be a typically Herodian concern and must have seemed to be a perfect way to discredit Jesus. If he said "yes" to the taxes, he would lose favor with the people; if he said "no," then they would have grounds for a civil accusation against him to the Roman authorities.

People of the Land. The general population of Palestine—the vast majority of the people, in other words—belonged to none of the above parties. Called the *am ha-aretz* ("people of the land"—obviously not a compliment) by their richer and more theologically astute contemporaries, they were the peasant classes whose primary concern in life was survival. They hadn't the time for the Pharisees' squabbles about the Law or the Sadducees' and Herodians' political intrigues. Interestingly, it seems Jesus drew most of his followers from this group, probably because they were otherwise without hope and had nothing to lose as far as worldly power and wealth were concerned.

So What Was Jesus?

As you can see from even the brief survey above, Judaism in the time of Jesus exhibited a tremendous variety of beliefs and practices. Now it's time to ask the obvious question: Where does Jesus fit in with all of this? Was he a member of any of these groups, or was he a lone wolf who held himself aloof from all of them?

We can dispense with some of the categories right away. It's obvious that Jesus was not a Zealot, since he never advocated the violent overthrow of Rome and taught such non-Zealot concepts as loving your enemies. Likewise, he clearly wasn't a Herodian (he had no wealth or political influence); and he didn't belong to the priestly class, so he wasn't a Sadducee. Just these few observations narrow the possibilities considerably.

Was he an Essene? Many have tried to make this case, even claiming that Jesus figures prominently in the Dead Sea Scrolls, which is odd, since he isn't named in them a single time. The claim that both Jesus and his cousin John the Baptist were Essenes rests mainly on the fact that they don't fit readily into the other categories and that both of them strongly, at times, denounced mainstream Judaism (Luke 3.7–14; Matt 23.1–39). However, remember that the Old Testament prophets did much the same, and that didn't mean they were members of any particular separatist movement. In reality, there are quite a few contrasts between the theology of both John and Jesus compared to that of the Essenes, making it highly unlikely that either of them was part of this group.[2]

---

[2]See the first chapter in *Jesus and the Dead Sea Scrolls*, ed. J. H. Charlesworth (Doubleday, 1992).

That leaves only two possibilities: Either Jesus was a Pharisee, or he was simply one of the "people of the land," not to be identified with any of the other known groups.

Because of the evident hostility between Jesus and the Pharisees, as amply attested in the Gospels, we are perhaps too readily inclined to conclude that he had almost nothing in common with them. However, according to the Gospels, that assumption is entirely wrong. Jesus shared with the Pharisees a strong respect for the Law (Matt 5.17–19), even though he charged them with not fulfilling the spirit of it (Matt 5.20; 23.16–26). In Matthew 23.1–3 we find a perhaps surprising respect for the religious leadership of the Pharisees: "The scribes and Pharisees sit on Moses' seat, so practice and observe whatever they tell you—but not what they do. For they preach, but do not practice." Notice it is the Pharisees' failure to live up to their teachings—not the teachings themselves—with which Jesus took issue. Likewise, Jesus sided with the Pharisees against the Sadducees in defending the concept of resurrection and afterlife (Luke 20.27–40), and he shared their belief in the existence of angels and demons (for angels, see Luke 20.36; concerning demons, see the numerous accounts of Jesus' casting them out). And we shouldn't overlook that Jesus at times interacted with Pharisees socially and on fairly friendly terms (Luke 7.36; 11.37; 14.1), that "some Pharisees" warned Jesus that Herod was out to kill him (Luke 13.31), that Jesus commended a scribe (presumably also a Pharisee) as being "not far from the kingdom of God" (Mark 12.28–34), and that it was a Pharisee who spoke up in defense of Jesus and who, along with another member of the Sanhedrin (Jewish ruling council), saw to the burial of his body (John 3.1; 7.45–52; 19.39–40).

This is not to suggest at all that Jesus ever "held membership" (if there was such a thing) in the group known as Pharisees. It is simply to say that many of his beliefs were parallel with theirs and much closer to theirs than to any of the other known groups, except perhaps for the people of the land.

We must remember, too, that Jesus differed from the Pharisees in significant ways, as revealed especially in the numerous "conflict stories" found in the Synoptic Gospels. For example, whereas the Pharisees were zealous to protect the Sabbath day by forbidding numerous activities not specified in the Law of Moses, Jesus placed the observance of the Sabbath as secondary to the meeting of human need (Mark 2.23–3.6; Luke 13.10–17). Likewise, he thoroughly criticized the Pharisees' dietary scruples by maintaining that it isn't what a person eats that makes him or her unclean, but what comes from within (Mark 7.14–23). And he showed no regard at all for their oral tradition when it conflicted with the intent of the Law of Moses.

So, although Jesus' own views in many respects closely paralleled those of the Pharisees, it isn't likely that he was one of them. For one thing, his family background (see Chapter Three) and tendency to identify with the poor and outcast (a very non-Pharisaic thing to do; see Luke 15.1–2) would argue against this. So we should probably conclude that Jesus was one of the common people—but in a very uncommon way. We should not at all think this meant that Jesus came from anything like a secular Jewish background. Quite to the contrary, his parents are described as devout, observant Jews themselves, as seen mostly in the stories of his birth (Matt 1–2; Luke 1–2).

So, rather than trying to understand Jesus apart from his Jewish background, it makes far more sense to learn all we can about that background and then to understand Jesus in relation to it— doesn't it? After all, Jesus the Messiah was first of all Jesus the Jew.

Think About It

1. How is the "criterion of dissimilarity" bound to lead to a warped picture of who Jesus was? Why do you think scholars thought (think, in some instances) that this criterion would lead to a better understanding of Jesus?

2. Read one of the Gospels and make note of all of the indications of Jesus' "Jewishness." How does this change or enhance your understanding of him?

3. Why do you think Jesus participated in the synagogue, even though it was a later development in Judaism and not taught or described in the Old Testament? What does this suggest about his relationship to mainstream Judaism?

4. Read Mark 7. What lay behind Jesus' disagreements with the Jewish practices that are described there?

5. If Jesus had more in common with the Pharisees than with other Jewish groups, why do you think he was so often in conflict with them and less so with the others?

6. Why would the Sadducees have been particularly offended at Jesus' act known as the "cleansing of the temple" (Mark 11.15–19, 27–28)?

7. Do you think it is still true that Jesus appeals more to the "common people" (lower socio-economic classes) in society than to those with more wealth and power? Why or why not?

5

Who Did Jesus Claim to Be?

Watch Those Presuppositions!

I once attended a lecture by a renowned New Testament scholar on the topic "Was Jesus God?" The auditorium was packed with people who were eager to hear this great man's thoughts about such a crucial question. He began by saying that, in order to answer this question, we must first eliminate from consideration everything in the Gospel of John, since John is the Gospel which most strongly emphasizes Jesus' divine nature. Next, he said, we must discard any other statements or other indications in the entire New Testament that might point to a divine Jesus, since these were obviously the creations of the early church and did not go back to Jesus himself. Then, we were told, we can ask the question "Was Jesus God?" Well, you can imagine what conclusion he reached. Beginning with such negative presuppositions and eliminating all evidence to the contrary, he naturally found the negative answer he was seeking.

One of the major historical issues surrounding the person of Jesus of Nazareth has to do with his own sense of identity: Who did he think he was? And who did he claim to be? Now, this is a different question than whether or not he *was* who he claimed to be. There have always been detractors who have claimed that he wasn't Israel's Messiah, the Son of God, God-in-the-flesh, etc. But the most recent denial of Jesus as being any or all of these is different. Now the claim is that he never *said* he was and didn't see himself in these ways.

Where, then, you might ask, did such notions as those expressed in the Gospels come from? The answer, we are told, is that these are things that the later church eventually came to *believe* about Jesus, and so they wrote them into the Gospels to make it sound as if these were Jesus' claims also. In other words, according to these critics, Jesus never did many of the things the Gospels claim he did, and he never claimed that he was what Christianity later made him out to be.

As with everything else about Jesus, the Gospels are our primary sources of information. Those who reject them as reliable conclude that we can know almost nothing about Jesus. Naturally, this leaves Jesus open to all sorts of interpretations. Interpreters who take this approach usually begin with a preconceived idea of who Jesus was, then scour the Gospels to eliminate everything that doesn't fit their already-painted portrait of him. This was certainly the case with the "Jesus Seminar," who began their research into Jesus' sayings by stating that they would "rescue" Jesus from the church and what it had come to believe about him.[1] And guess what? The "Jesus" they came up with is a very different one from the person portrayed in the New Testament.

In all fairness, we are all prone to see the evidence as tilted in the direction of what we already believe. We all have our presuppositions, and those presuppositions often cause us to accept or reject evidence accordingly. There are those who claim to be entirely objective, but this is impossible. We all have our own slant on things, especially where something as important as the identity of Jesus is concerned. Since we are incapable of being "presuppositionless," the best we can do is be honest about what our presuppositions are, rather than claiming omniscient objectivity and speaking as if our view of the evidence is without problems of its own.

I have already said in Chapter One that I accept the Gospels as reliable sources of information for Jesus, not simply on the grounds of faith but also of history. It seems to me that it remains for those who think otherwise to offer their evidence to the contrary.

---

[1] R. W. Funk, *Honest to Jesus* (Harper/San Francisco, 1996), 300. See the critique of this approach in James D. G. Dunn, *A New Perspective on Jesus* (Baker Publishing Group, 2005), 21–22.

But time and again the Gospels have been shown to be rooted in history and to be factually correct in many respects. Why, then, should we assume that they are incorrect in what they say about the claims of Jesus? Whether we choose to believe those claims or not is another matter. It is important to understand that historical data by itself can neither confirm nor deny spiritual claims. But let's allow the evidence to speak for itself.

For example, the way Luke begins his Gospel shows that he writes as a conscious historian, someone who has sifted the information available to him and now presents it for the benefit of someone named Theophilus. Listen to his opening words:

> Inasmuch as many have undertaken to compile a narrative of the things which have been accomplished among us, just as those who from the beginning were eyewitnesses and ministers of the word have delivered them to us, it seemed good to me also, having followed all things closely for some time past, to write an orderly account for you, most excellent Theophilus, that you may have certainty concerning the things you have been taught. (Luke 1.1–4)

Luke then proceeds to open his narrative with a historical reference: "In the days of Herod, king of Judea..." And remember Luke 3.1–2. There is no "once-upon-a-time" quality to his work.

This preface to Luke's Gospel is significant on a number of counts. Notice first of all that Luke has done his homework. He is aware of "many" attempts to write the story of Jesus and has read them, since he contrasts his own work as being an "orderly" account. (What did he think was "disorderly" about the others? We don't know. We don't even know what the others were, but evidently they were not Matthew, Mark, and John, since Luke's account parallels those of Matthew and Mark so closely, and John was by most calculations not written yet.) Also, Luke honestly admits that he is not an eyewitness of these things, but he has apparently talked with those who were ("those who from the beginning were eyewitnesses and ministers of the word have delivered them to us"). And pay attention to Luke's stated purpose in writing: "that you may *have certainty* concerning the things you have been taught." Whether Theophilus was already a Christian or not, we can't tell. He had some knowledge of Christianity, but Luke obviously felt it was inadequate in some way, and he wanted to give Theophilus the facts. (Read also Acts 1.1, keeping in mind that Acts is Luke's "Volume 2": "In the first book, O Theophilus, I have dealt with all that Jesus began to do and teach…") So Luke clearly intended to tell us *what happened.* Anyone who questions this bears the burden of proof that Luke was either lying or simply didn't know what he was talking about.

The same things could be said of the other Gospels, although they do not state their historical intentions as clearly as does Luke. But none of them tells the story of Jesus in a historical vacuum. And the early church accepted them all as factual accounts of who Jesus was and what he did. If we are to discard almost 2000 years of consistent Christian belief about these things, we must do better than simply claim objectivity (and omniscience) for ourselves while denying it to the Gospel writers, who lived in much closer proximity to the events and had access to eyewitnesses, even if some of them were not eyewitnesses themselves.

That being said, and acknowledging our presuppositions about the Gospels and their historical validity, let's see what they record Jesus as saying about himself.

King of the Jews and Representative of the True Israel

Some of Jesus' claims were not verbal but are evident in specific things he did to reveal his identity in connection with various promises from the Old Testament. These may be thought of as "acted parables."

For example, Mark 3.13–19 records Jesus' appointment of his twelve apostles (although they aren't called that in Mark 3). All four Gospels acknowledge that Jesus had an inner circle of 12 followers (in addition to many others) and that he spent much of his public ministry teaching and training these men to take the lead once he was no longer with them. But have you ever wondered why he appointed *12?* Why not 10, or 20, or any other number? And Acts 1.15–26 says that after Jesus' ascension into heaven the remaining band of disciples (numbering about 120) chose Matthias to replace Judas, who had defected from his apostolic role. So the number 12 was kept intact. However, as the remainder of the original 12 began to die out (as recorded in Acts 12.1–2, with the death of James), they were *not* replaced as Judas had been. Once again, there seems to be something significant about the number 12.

There is. It is clear that Jesus was appointing 12 to lead the new people of God (later called the church), just as the nation of Israel had its 12 Patriarchs (the 12 sons of Jacob), each of whom was leader of a particular tribe. Jesus evidently saw himself as creating a "renewed Israel," and therefore it was necessary to have 12 authoritative leaders for it. (See Rev 21.12–14 for confirmation of this interpretation; also note the significance of the number 12 and its multiples throughout Rev as a symbol for the people of God.)

If Jesus appointed the 12 apostles as leaders of the new Israel, then it is evident that Jesus saw himself as Israel's new king. That he did is further evidenced by the way he entered Jerusalem for the last time. Matthew 21.1–5 says he rode into the city on a donkey. This would hardly be the normal way for a king to enter his capital! What was Jesus doing, and why? Matthew makes it clear that this was not merely an accidental detail, because of the precise preparations that were made for Jesus to ride this particular animal into Jerusalem. The reason becomes obvious when you read Zechariah 9.9:

> Rejoice greatly, O daughter of Zion!
>   Shout aloud, O daughter of Jerusalem!
> behold, your king is coming to you;
>   righteous and having salvation is he,
> humble and mounted on a donkey,
>   on a colt, the foal of a donkey.

Jesus' choice of transport into the holy city was a conscious fulfillment of this prophecy of Israel's coming King. And, by entering the city in this way, Jesus was claiming to be that King.

Did Jesus say anything that would confirm this portrait of him as King and national representative of Israel? Listen to Mark 10.42–45:

> And Jesus called them to him and said to them, "You know that those who are considered rulers of the Gentiles lord it over them, and their great ones exercise authority over them. But it shall not be so among you. But whoever would be great among you must be your servant, and whoever would be first among you must be slave of all. For even the Son of man came not to be served but to serve, and to give his life as a ransom for many."

That last sentence indicates that Jesus saw himself as the "Suffering Servant" (who would give his life as a ransom for others) spoken of in the "Servant Songs" of Isaiah 42.1–4 and 52.13–53.12. But notice especially Isaiah 49.3: "You are my servant, Israel, in whom I will be glorified." In this verse, at least, the "Servant" is identified as the nation itself. And in Mark 10.45 Jesus takes that role upon himself. So not only does he claim to be Israel's king, but also the representative of the true (newly-constituted) Israel.

Messiah

As indicated earlier, "Messiah" is from a Hebrew word which means "the Anointed One." In the Old Testament kings, prophets, judges, and others were often anointed to render special service to God. Eventually, the belief arose that one unique Messiah would come—one who would fully and finally deliver Israel from all her oppressions. The root of this belief is found in 2 Samuel 7, which tells us of King David's desire to build a house for God. Through a prophet named Nathan, God responded that he didn't need David to build him a house and hadn't asked for one. (Was David getting the "big head," to think he could build a house for the Lord?) Rather, the Lord said, he would build a house for David. But God wasn't talking about a dwelling, but rather a lineage, a line of descendants (as when we speak of the "House of Windsor," meaning a certain line of rulers) to sit on Israel's throne forever, beginning with David's "offspring." Not only is this "offspring" further identified as David's son, but God said, "I will be to him a father, and he shall be to me a son, and I will establish the throne of his kingdom forever." Now all of this could have been simply speaking of David's heir to the throne, Solomon. But then God spoke of "forever," and it becomes clear that there are some promises here that were not fulfilled in the reign of Solomon. They seem to point forward to someone else. This "someone else" came to be identified in Israelite thought with a coming Messiah. During the darkest days of Israel's history, the longing for a deliverer to come continued to give hope to the people, that eventually God would act by sending this Anointed One to redeem his people.

So how does Jesus figure into this? Remember first of all that Jesus is repeatedly called in the New Testament "Jesus Christ." "Christ" is from the Greek word *christos*, which is equivalent to the Hebrew word for "Messiah" ("Anointed One"). So, when the New Testament writers speak of Jesus as "Jesus Christ," they aren't giving us his first and last names. His name is Jesus, and he is being claimed as Israel's long-awaited Messiah.

On one very important occasion, recorded in Matthew 16.13–17, Jesus quizzed his disciples about who people thought he was. "Some say John the Baptist, others say Elijah, and others Jeremiah or one of the prophets," they replied. Notice that none of these were derogatory identifications; all showed that people held Jesus in high esteem during his ministry in Galilee. But they weren't the full truth either, so Jesus pressed a bit harder: "But who do *you* say that I am?" After having been with them for some time now, what did they think about him? What conclusions were they reaching? While it was naturally important what other people thought, it was absolutely crucial what the apostles thought. Peter spoke for the group: "You are the Christ, the Son of the living God." The 12 had concluded that Jesus was in fact Israel's long-awaited Messiah. Notice Jesus' reply: "Blessed are you, Simon Bar-Jona [that is, "son of Jonah"]! For flesh and blood has not revealed this to you, but my Father who is in heaven." Notice that Jesus concurred with Peter's statement about his identity and, true to God's promise to David, referred to God as "my Father."

Equally important is the occasion when, as he was being interrogated by the Jewish authorities, Jesus was asked directly, "Are you the Christ (Messiah)?" All three Synoptic Gospels record this question or some variation of it (Matt 26.63–64; Mark 14.61–62; Luke 22.67–71). In Matthew, Jesus' reply is "You have said so." Mark has "I am." Luke has "You say that I am." Now to us these may not seem to be all the same answer, but in each instance the Jewish authorities took Jesus' reply as a positive response. The differences are probably due to the fact that Jesus was speaking Aramaic and each Gospel author paraphrases in Greek. It may also indicate that Jesus was acknowledging his identity but was deliberately vague about his answer, since he knew that what he meant by it was not what they meant. Their question probably meant something like, "Do you claim to be the political-military deliverer we've been waiting for?" Jesus was in fact claiming to be the Promised One, but in a different sense; he would deliver his people from their greatest enemy—sin—and without the trappings of royalty and military might.

Another obvious claim to Messiahship occurs in Luke 4.16–21. Jesus was attending the synagogue in his hometown of Nazareth. When it came time for the portion of the service in which a passage from the Prophets was to be read, Jesus stood up to read, and the scroll of Isaiah was handed to him. He opened it to the place where Isaiah had written,

> The Spirit of the Lord is upon me,
>   because he has anointed me to proclaim good news to the poor.
> He has sent me to proclaim liberty to the captives
>   and recovering of sight to the blind,
>   to set at liberty those who are oppressed, to proclaim the year
>   of the Lord's favor.

The reading was Isaiah 61.1–2, a text which Jews regarded as a prophecy of the coming age of the Messiah. But it was what happened next that changed the tone of the whole event: "And he began to say to them, 'Today this scripture has been fulfilled in your hearing.'" In other words, Jesus was claiming that the Messianic Age had begun with him, that he was in fact the one upon whom the Spirit of the Lord rested and who would preach good news to the poor, etc.

Son of Man

You may have noticed by this point that I haven't yet mentioned any texts in which Jesus himself *overtly* claimed to be the Messiah, although what we have looked at so far shows that he did think of himself in this way. But according to the Synoptics, Jesus preferred to call himself the "Son of Man." This was a somewhat ambiguous title. To refer to someone as the "son of" something was a typical Hebrew way to indicate that person's character. For example, Judas is called "the son of destruction" (John 17.12) because by his actions in betraying Jesus he stood condemned. One of the apostle Paul's companions was a man named Barnabas, which means "son of encouragement" (Acts 4:36), evidently because he was such an encouraging person to Paul as well as to others. So "Son of Man" could mean nothing more than "man-like" or "human being." We might leave it at that, but there is a text in Daniel 7.13–14 that suggests we shouldn't. Daniel relates a vision in which he saw "one like a son of man." We might conclude that he means simply "a human figure," but then comes verse 14: "And to him was given dominion and glory and a kingdom, that all peoples, nations, and languages should serve him; his dominion is an everlasting dominion, which shall not pass away, and his kingdom one that shall not be destroyed." Suddenly it becomes evident that "son of man" (at least in this text) doesn't mean just "human being." Because of this, some Jews believed that "Son of Man" was another title for the Messiah. So, when Jesus called himself "Son of Man," it probably caused people to wonder exactly what he meant by it. And that seems to be what Jesus wanted. It was a title that suggested the possibility of Messiahship but without coming right out and saying so.

But why wouldn't he just come right out and say, "I'm the Messiah!" if that's who he believed himself to be? For a very good reason. In First-Century Judaism there were many ideas of who and what the Messiah would be and do. Most of these centered on the idea of a militaristic leader who would overthrow Rome and re-establish Israel as a political entity. He would truly be "David's son" in the sense of being a great warrior-king, just as David had been. If Jesus had used overt messianic language about himself, or if he had encouraged others to do so, it could have had political repercussions that he preferred to avoid. There were always disgruntled and desperate Jews who were ready to follow almost anyone who claimed to be Messiah, but Jesus had no interest in starting an uprising, since that wasn't what his mission was about anyway. Also, he didn't want his disciples using this kind of terminology until at least *they* understood what he meant by it. This point is brought home with great force in Matthew 16.20–21, just after Peter's correct identification of Jesus as Messiah. "Then he strictly charged the disciples to tell no one that he was the Christ." Why? Because they didn't yet understand the true meaning of messiahship or the kind of Messiah he had come to be. "From that time Jesus began to show his disciples that he must go to Jerusalem and suffer many things from the elders and chief priests and scribes, and be killed, and on the third day be raised." It was best that they not call him Messiah until they understood that this Messiah was to suffer and die, not conquer and kill.

All of this meshes very well with what we know of Jewish political and messianic expectations in the time of Jesus. And it is clear that Jesus did, in fact, believe himself to be the Messiah, and claimed to be so in indirect ways, even if he preferred to call himself "Son of Man."

Son of God

You may recall that when Peter replied to Jesus' question in Matthew 16.15, his answer was two-fold: "You are the Christ, the Son of the living God." Likewise, the high priest at Jesus' "Jewish trial" said to him, "Tell us if you are the Christ, the Son of God" (Matt 26.63). In both cases Jesus answered in a manner that showed that he affirmed both his Messiahship and Sonship.

But let's go back a bit further, to Matthew 11.25–27.

At that time Jesus declared, "I thank you, Father, Lord of heaven and earth, that you have hidden these things from the wise and understanding and revealed them to little children; yes, Father, for such was your gracious will. All things have been handed over to me by my Father; and no one knows the Son except the Father, and no one knows the Father except the Son and anyone to whom the Son chooses to reveal him."

Here Jesus calls God "my Father" and claims that he is the exclusive Revealer of God. Another passage in the same vein is John 5.16–18. Jesus has just healed a lame man and is being persecuted by the Jewish authorities for "working" (i.e., healing) on the Sabbath. Jesus responds to this charge by declaring, "My Father is working still, and I am working," another claim to Sonship. But even more telling is what follows: "This was why the Jews were seeking all the more to kill him, because not only was he breaking the Sabbath, but he was even calling God his own Father, *making himself equal with God.*" So the Jewish authorities understood Jesus' claim to be God's Son to mean that he was "equal with God." Then, in John 10.30, Jesus makes this striking statement: "I and the Father are one." Although this isn't, as sometimes thought, a claim that Jesus and God are the same *being*, it is a claim that they are on the same level and are one in purpose, that what is true of one is true of the other.

Okay, so Jesus claimed to be God's Son. But what exactly does that mean? "Jesus is the Son of God" is one of the most common confessions of the Christian faith, but do we ever stop to ask what this phrase tells us? Especially, what did Jesus mean by it?

First, it is obvious that it indicates a unique relationship between Jesus and God. There is a general sense in which people and even angels are sometimes called "sons of God" in the Bible, but it is obvious in the preceding texts that Jesus is saying more than that. And it was obvious to his opponents; otherwise, they wouldn't have gotten so upset with him. In fact, the well-known words of John 3.16 say, "For God so loved the world that he gave his *only Son,* that whoever believes in him should not perish but have eternal life." The Greek word *monogenes* (sometimes translated as "only-begotten") means something like "unique," "one-and-only." So by calling himself God's Son, Jesus claimed a unique relationship with God.

Second, it is obvious that "Son of God" at least *implies* being on a par with God. This is evident both from Jesus' own words ("I and the Father are one") and also from the reaction of those who heard him ("because he made himself equal with God"). So the claim to Sonship becomes virtually a claim to deity itself. Jesus isn't just saying, "I'm really close to God." Rather, he seems to be saying, "God and I are of the same essence; we are one." This accounts for the fact that Jesus claimed the authority to forgive sins (Mark 2.5–7); that everyone would one day stand before him in judgment (Matt 7.22–23); and that he could unhesitatingly demand complete allegiance to himself (Matt 10.32–33).

Third, Jesus' claim to be God's Son indicates a conscious identification of himself with the promised "son of David" spoken of earlier in 2 Samuel 7, when God promised to build David a "house." And remember that God had also said, "I will be to him a father, and he shall be to me a son" (2 Sam 7.14). So the claim to be Son of God meshes with the claim to be the Messiah.[2]

Other Indications of Jesus' Self-Identity

So Jesus claimed to be Israel's Messiah, the Son of Man, and the Son of God. Are there any other things he said that would add to our understanding of who he thought he was, or that would support what we have already seen?

One peculiarity of Jesus' teachings as recorded in John's Gospel (5.19, 25; 6.26, 47, 53; 8.34, 58; etc.) is the way he would preface some of his more profound sayings with the words, "Truly, truly, I say to you" (in some translations, "Amen, amen, I say to you"). These words indicate a saying with great authority, one that is guaranteed by the character of the speaker himself. They suggest that Jesus saw his own teachings as having a self-authenticating quality. He didn't have to quote others; he just "quoted himself."

---

[2]See the statistical summary of the occurrence of various titles of Jesus in the New Testament in Craig A. Evans, *Fabricating Jesus* (InterVarsity Press, 2006), 191–193.

This is either an indication of a conviction of great authority or of extraordinary arrogance. If Jesus is who he said, it is obviously the former; if not, then it is clearly the latter.

Another striking claim of Jesus is found in Luke 6.1–5. Jesus and his disciples were passing through a grain field on the Sabbath. The disciples were hungry, so they quite naturally reached out and plucked some heads of grain and ate them. According to the rules of the Pharisees, who saw themselves as the guardians of the Law, this amounted to "work." So they criticized Jesus and his followers. (Were they following them around, looking for such things?) Jesus gave a two-fold response to their criticism. First, he pointed out that they didn't know their Bible very well, for in the Old Testament David and his men had done something equally "illegal" by going to the shrine at Nob, as they were running away from King Saul, and eating the "bread of the Presence," sacred loaves that were kept as an offering to God. So there was good precedent for "violating" the Sabbath laws when human need required it. Second, Jesus said something that must have sounded like blasphemy in their ears: "The Son of man is lord of the Sabbath." In other words, Jesus was claiming authority over one of Israel's most sacred institutions. Since the Sabbath was a divine institution established by God himself, this amounted to an unmistakable claim to deity.

On a similar note, Jesus' actions in "cleansing" the Temple (another of those "acted parables" I mentioned earlier) amounted to a claim of authority over it. Jesus was not cleansing the sacred house for further and better use, but rather he was pronouncing divine judgment on it and on the system it represented. It's not at all surprising that following this episode the chief priests, scribes, and elders came to him and demanded, "Tell us by what authority you do these things, or who it is that gave you this authority" (Luke 20.2). Only someone who believed that he was acting on the authority of God would dare do such a thing.

We'll conclude with a final example. In John 8 Jesus engaged in a heated exchange with some of the Jews. They accused him of being demon-possessed and a Samaritan (both extreme insults), and he accused them of acting in accord with the character of their father, the devil. Finally, they based their defense on their relation to "our father Abraham" (8.53). Jesus responded, "Your father Abraham rejoiced that he would see my day. He saw it and was glad" (8.56). This brought forth the astonished question, "You are not yet fifty years old, and have you seen Abraham?" Then Jesus said something that caused them to pick up stones to kill him: "Truly, truly ('amen, amen'), I say to you, before Abraham was, I am" (8.58). Two things are important here. First, Jesus was claiming to have existed even before Abraham, getting awfully close to a claim to deity. Second, he ended his sentence with the words *ego eimi*: "I am." In these words any Jew who knew his Bible would have instantly been reminded of Moses and the burning bush in Exodus 3. When Moses asked the Lord to tell who it was who was sending him to demand from Pharaoh the release of the Israelites, God responded, "Tell them 'I Am' has sent you." And this became the covenant name by which God was known to his people from then on: "I Am." And now here was Jesus saying, "*I* am." No wonder they picked up the rocks! This was either profound truth or utter blasphemy.

"Who did Jesus claim to be?" may sound like a simple question, but as you can see it has a complex answer. But the message is clear: Jesus believed himself to be the Messiah of Israel, the apocalyptic Son of Man, and God's own Son. Even those who do not believe these things to be true about him should acknowledge, on the basis of the evidence, that this is what he claimed about himself. Once that is clear, then we must face the question that Jesus asked his disciples so long ago: "But who do *you* say that I am?"

Think About It

1. Why are presuppositions so important in our attempt to understand who Jesus was? What are your own presuppositions? Why is it impossible to be "presuppositionless"?

2. What kinds of things did Jesus do that pointed to his self-understanding?

3. What kinds of things did Jesus say that pointed to his self-understanding?

4. Explain the concept of a coming Messiah in Judaism. How did the popular conception of this individual affect the way Jews thought about Jesus in his own time?

5. What claims did Jesus make that point to his self-understanding?

6. Which titles of Jesus do you find most helpful in thinking about him? Least helpful?

7. Why do you think the New Testament gives so many different titles to Jesus? Would it have been more helpful if there were only one or maybe two?

6

Why and How Did Jesus Die?

Naturally, the death of Jesus is central to the Bible's message about him. And it is one of the most firmly established historical facts about him, that he died by crucifixion at the hands of Pontius Pilate on the insistence of the Jewish authorities, as we learned in our first chapter. But what else can we know about his death? What exactly did it mean to be crucified? And why was this done to Jesus? In attempting to answer these historical questions, we get help from both the Bible itself and also from sources outside the Bible.

How: Death by Crucifixion
Mel Gibson's 2004 film, "The Passion of the Christ," brought home vividly the brutality and inhumanity of death by crucifixion. With all of the discussion that took place after the film's release, it was surprising to me how many people complained of the violence portrayed in the movie. As one who has studied the crucifixion for many years, my response was "What did you expect?" But I suppose it shows just how little we really understand about how Jesus died.

Crucifixion was a form of torture and execution that was not invented by the Romans, but was "perfected" by them (if one may use that term for such a hideous act). It originally involved impaling the dead bodies of slain enemies on sharpened stakes or poles, leaving them exposed to the animals and elements as a means of showing both victory over and contempt for the conquered. Later, someone got the brilliant idea of impaling people while still alive.

The Romans took this awful method and "refined" it into a prolonged death by either nailing or tying their victims to poles or crosses, leaving them to a slow, agonizing death. (One of our most descriptive English words for pain is "excruciating," which is derived from the Latin phrase *ex crucis*—"from the cross.")

Death by crucifixion usually resulted from shock, secondary infection, exposure, exhaustion, suffocation, etc. There was nothing about crucifixion itself that would cause immediate death. If the victim was tied to the cross, then there would be no wounds at all, except for those that might have been administered in the beating that sometimes (not always) preceded crucifixion. Even when the hands were nailed to the wood, it was done by inserting the nail (actually a slender spike) carefully between the bones of the wrist. This had the effect of providing a bone structure to support the weight of the victim's body while on the cross (nailed palms would probably not have withstood such weight), and also avoided the rupturing of any major blood vessels that could result in bleeding to death. So the victim would be left to die, a process that often took several days.

In Jesus' case, however, death came relatively quickly (approximately six hours, according to the Gospels). This suggests that Jesus probably died due to cardiac arrest or a rupture of the heart, as suggested by John 19.34 (and with which many medical experts agree): "But one of the soldiers pierced his side with a spear, and at once there came out blood and water." The "blood and water" probably resulted from the separation of the serum and solid particles of the blood following Jesus' death. His death was undoubtedly hastened by the fact that he had been scourged prior to crucifixion. Scourging was itself a gruesome process. The whip consisted of several leather thongs with bits of bone, metal, or glass woven into them, so the flesh would be torn with each stroke. Some ancient writers comment that, in cases of severe scourging, the internal organs of the victim sometimes became visible through the back. Needless to say, many people died from the scourging alone.

In the case of the two criminals who were crucified with Jesus, death resulted from suffocation. People were usually crucified with their legs bent at the knee, with the feet either nailed or tied to a block of wood. This allowed the victim to push down with the legs in order to take air into the diaphragm. After hours of the exhaustion of having one's arms stretched out and bearing the weight of the entire body, this was the only way to breathe, as painful as it would be to push down on nailed feet. John 19.31–33 explains that the Jewish authorities asked Pilate to break the legs of the three crucified men to hasten their deaths so their bodies could be removed and not remain on the crosses during the Passover Sabbath. Breaking the legs meant the victim could no longer breathe by pushing down on the legs, and death usually followed in a matter of minutes. Jesus' legs would have been broken also, but the soldiers saw that he was already dead. One of them thrust a spear into his side just to make sure.

Crucifixion involved not only intense physical pain but shame and humiliation as well. The Romans knew how to get full propaganda value out of the act of executing criminals, so crucifixions almost always took place in very public places, such as beside well-traveled roads into and out of cities. (In the case of Jesus' crucifixion, we don't know the exact location, although several have been suggested.) The charge for which the person was being executed would be written on a placard and placed above the condemned man's head so that everyone who passed by would know what brought this about and would think twice before doing it himself. All three Synoptic Gospels mention the inscription over Jesus' head, which read, "The King of the Jews." John 19.19–22 adds that it was written in Hebrew (probably Aramaic, the common dialect of Palestine), in Latin (the official language of the Roman Empire), and in Greek (the common language in use all around the Mediterranean). Whether or not this was always done in the three languages, we don't know. But Pilate made sure everyone could read it. John also records the Jews' objection and their attempt to get Pilate to re-word the inscription to read, "This man *said*, I am King of the Jews." But Pilate took a kind of weak revenge against his Jewish subjects (whom he despised anyway) for forcing him into an execution that he wanted nothing to do with, and said, "What I have written, I have written." Of course, the Gospel writers naturally saw the inscription as a confession of the truth about Jesus, that he truly was "King of the Jews."

Because crucifixion was such a humiliating way to die, it was reserved for the lowest of criminals and was not normally used on Roman citizens (although history does record a few exceptions). This explains why, according to the early Christian historian Eusebius,[1] the apostle Paul—a Roman citizen—was beheaded rather than crucified. Peter, on the other hand, being merely a Galilean peasant, was crucified (see the somewhat cryptic reference to the manner of Peter's death in John 21.18–19). The humiliation of crucifixion also helps us understand the mockery Jesus received both before and during his crucifixion. How could anyone who was chosen by God possibly end up in such a sorry state, especially one who claimed to be a king? (See Luke 23.32–38; Mark 15.16–32; Matt 27.27–44; Heb 12.2; Phil 2.8–9.)

The shame of crucifixion explains why, to many ancient people who first heard the story of Jesus, the cross became, to use Paul's term, a "stumbling block"[2] (1 Cor 1.23; Gal 5.11). This may seem strange to those of us who sing songs such as "The Old Rugged Cross" and "In the Cross of Christ I Glory," but it's perfectly understandable. From a pagan point of view, it made no sense that any sort of "victory" could be gained or good accomplished by someone's being crucified. From a Jewish point of view, the cross itself ruled out Jesus as possibly being the Messiah. After all, Deuteronomy 21.23 pronounces a curse on everyone who was "hanged on a tree." (See Josh 8.29, where being hanged on a tree after death was an indication of utter defeat and humiliation.) And surely God's Messiah could not be a cursed person! This posed something of a theological problem for the early church as they proclaimed a Messiah both crucified and risen. Paul addresses it in Galatians 3.13–14, where he actually quotes the curse from

---

[1] *Church History* 2.25.5.

[2] From the Greek word *skandalon*, which originally meant a trap, then came to mean a cause for offense. Our English word "scandal" comes from this word, and so we often hear the expression "the scandal of the cross," based on Paul's comments cited above.

Deuteronomy 21, but explains that "Christ redeemed us from the curse of the law [i.e., our inability to keep it—Gal 3.10–12], by becoming a curse for us..." Paul does not deny the accursedness of Jesus' situation, but he insists that Jesus was taking our "curse" upon himself by submitting to death by crucifixion.

Paul's most eloquent defense of the cross occurs in 1 Corinthians 1.18–25, where he acknowledges that "the word of the cross is folly to those who are perishing, but to us who are being saved it is the power of God." He goes on to say that, although the Jews demanded "signs" (absolute proof of Jesus' identity) and Greeks looked for "wisdom" (probably a philosophical system that made sense to them), he continued to proclaim "Christ crucified, a stumbling block to Jews and folly to Gentiles, but to those who are called, both Jews and Greeks, Christ the power of God and the wisdom of God. For the foolishness of God is wiser than men, and the weakness of God is stronger than men." While the cross might not make sense to unbelievers, Paul says, God has provided in it another way of knowing God and his love—the way of the cross. And we have to ask whether or not the cross remains a stumbling block to many people now, just as in the First Century AD, because it in no way appeals to human reason and pride, and because we prefer not to think about the reality of sin and how to remove it.

So what we know of the manner of Jesus' death is entirely consistent with our information about Roman crucifixion and with how both Jews and Gentiles would have perceived it.

It is significant that none of the New Testament authors goes into any of the gory details of the process of crucifixion or of Jesus' agony on the cross. They describe his execution with the sparest of statements: "And they crucified him" (Mark 15.24; see also Matt 27.35; Luke 23.33; John 19.18). This is consistent with the practice of most ancient writers, who seldom mention the details of crucifixion, apparently thinking it would be in bad taste to do so. In the case of the authors of the Gospels, the reasons for not giving the details are not difficult to understand. For one thing, their earliest readers knew all too well what a crucifixion looked like, since, as we have already pointed out, executions normally took place in full public view. The mention of the word "cross" to them did not conjure up images of an architectural detail for a house of worship or a piece of jewelry; it was, plainly and simply, an instrument of death. But a second reason for their reticence has to do with their theological interests in telling the story of Jesus. For them what was of greatest importance were not the details of death but who it was who died and why he did so. And to that we now turn our attention.

Why?

Having explored the question of how Jesus died, we now need to ask an even more important question: *Why* did he die? What did he do to bring about such a horrible death with all its attendant suffering? Or did he do anything at all to cause it? Is there any blame to be fixed for Jesus' death, and if so, on whom?

In attempting to answer this question of why he died, we need to come at it from two angles, the historical and the theological. Historically, what were the circumstances that brought about his death? Theologically, what was the reason that he "had" to die, as he himself said (Luke 9.22; 24.45–47)? What did his death accomplish?

Historical Reasons

First, let's examine the historical reasons for Jesus' death. Mark 3.1–6 reports that early in his Galilean ministry, Jesus had irritated the religious authorities by asking them questions they couldn't answer and by exposing their lack of spiritual perception. One Sabbath day in the synagogue, Jesus encountered a man with a withered hand. The religious leaders, indifferent toward the man's plight, were watching to see whether or not Jesus would "violate" the Sabbath by healing him. Jesus presented the man to them as a living example of human need and asked them if it were lawful on the Sabbath to do good or to do harm, to save life or to kill. Not wanting to appear hard-hearted yet not wanting to violate their own rules, they remained silent. Jesus was angered and grieved over their hardness of heart and healed the man.

Naturally, this made the Pharisees look bad, and Mark says they "immediately held counsel with the Herodians against him, how to destroy him." The depth of their resentment toward Jesus is revealed in the fact that these two groups joined forces against him, since normally they were seriously at odds with one another. The Pharisees were the Jewish sect who advocated strict observance of the Law and who opposed the imposition of Greco-Roman culture on the Jewish people. The Herodians, as their name implies, were the wealthy backers of the policies of Herod, which included playing ball with the Romans. The two groups despised each other but were united in their opposition to Jesus. So, even at this early stage of his public life, the handwriting was on the wall: The religious authorities were out to get Jesus.

This situation only worsened once Jesus arrived in Jerusalem during the final week of his life. Matthew 22.15–46 records a series of clashes between Jesus and representatives of the various groups within Judaism. They continually tried to trap him into saying something worthy of arrest and execution, but he repeatedly evaded their efforts and continued to expose the shallowness of their spiritual thinking. In the first such encounter, the Pharisees and Herodians (again) laid what they must have thought was an inescapable trap for him. They asked him about the legality of paying taxes to Caesar. If Jesus affirmed the obligation to pay taxes, then he would quickly lose favor with the people, who despised their Roman overlords. If he said taxes should be withheld, they could bring a civil charge against him with the Roman authorities as an insurrectionist. But Jesus' answer left them with nothing to say and must have proved somewhat embarrassing: "Render... to Caesar the things that are Caesar's, and to God the things that are God's."

Representatives of other Jewish groups tried their hand at trapping Jesus, but to no avail. Finally, the chief priests and elders of the people put their heads together to figure out how to arrest Jesus and kill him without causing a riot among the people (Matt 26.3–5). They had to be careful because it was Passover season. Jerusalem was swollen with pilgrims to the great festival, and it was always a time of heightened messianic expectations and unrest. It wouldn't take much to set off a serious disturbance among the people, many of whom believed Jesus to be a prophet, if not the Messiah himself. If the religious leaders allowed such a thing to happen, the Romans would step in and deal with everyone severely. So they had to be careful.

However, it wasn't only Jesus' verbal encounters with the religious leaders that led to his death. Upon his arrival in Jerusalem he had gone to the Temple and driven out the money-changers and animal-sellers who had set up shop in the "Court of the Gentiles" (Mark 11.15–19). What is usually referred to as the "cleansing" of the Temple was a bold act that infuriated the religious leaders, particularly the chief priests and scribes who had control of the Temple and its activities. Jesus' actions indicated not only a judgment on their management of the Temple and its affairs but also a claim to have authority over it. But Mark also adds that "all the multitude"—i.e., the crowds of ordinary worshipers—"were astonished at his teaching." This sway over the people made Jesus a very dangerous man in the eyes of the Jewish authorities.

Another contributing factor in Jesus' eventual execution was a parable he told about a vineyard. It may have seemed like an innocent enough story on the surface, but it had ominous overtones, especially given the climate of the moment. We call it the Parable of the Wicked Tenants (Matt 21.33–41; also Mark 12.1–12; Luke 20.9–19). It's a story about a man who planted a vineyard, leased it out to sharecroppers, then went away to another country. When he sent servants to get his rightful share of the crop, they were beaten and some were killed by the tenants. A second attempt brought the same result. Finally, he sent his own son, thinking the tenants would respect him and give up their resistance. Instead, they killed him, thinking that with the heir out of the way the vineyard would somehow become theirs. At the conclusion of the parable, Jesus asked, "When therefore the owner of the vineyard comes, what will he do to those tenants?" Without hesitation they responded, "He will put those wretches to a miserable death, and let out the vineyard to other tenants who will give him the fruits in their seasons." The significance of this parable and their response to it lies in the fact that in the Old Testament Israel was frequently described by the prophets as God's "vineyard" (Isa 5.1–7; Jer 2.21). So the idea that the vineyard could be taken away and given to others was an affront to Jewish nationalism and especially a threat to its leaders. In verse 43 Jesus says exactly that: "Therefore I tell you, the kingdom of God will be taken away from you and given to a people producing its fruits." The impact on the religious leaders was immediate: "When the chief priests and the Pharisees heard his parables, they perceived that he was speaking about them. And although they were seeking to arrest him, they feared the crowds, because they held him to be a prophet" (Matt 21.45–46).

Eventually Jesus was arrested with the help of one of his own men, Judas Iscariot. John 18.31 says that it was not lawful for the Jews to execute anyone without the consent of the Romans, so they needed to find a charge against Jesus that would stick before delivering him to Pilate for trial. (This doesn't mean they never violated that law—see Acts 7.54–8.1—but this was a mob action and not a legal execution.) Matthew 26.57–68 says that Jesus, following his arrest in Gethsemane, was taken to the house of Caiaphas the high priest, where he was questioned by an apparently impromptu gathering of Jewish religious leaders. The upshot of this hearing is that Jesus was condemned on the religious charge of blasphemy. It is often assumed that this was because he claimed to be the Messiah, but this is unlikely. After all, many people were expecting the Messiah, and someone had to be the one. So a claim to messiahship in and of itself was not a religious crime. According to 26.64–65, the charge of blasphemy resulted from Jesus' statement that he was not only the Messiah but that they would see him "seated at the right hand of Power [i.e., God], and coming on the clouds of heaven." This obvious claim to divine status caused the high priest to call for an immediate verdict: "He deserves death."

The next step on Jesus' path to execution was his trial before Pilate. The religious authorities realized that Pilate couldn't care less about their charge of blasphemy. So they accused Jesus of being a rebel leader (Luke 23.1–5). Specifically, they accused him of forbidding the payment of taxes to Caesar (which, remember, he had not done) and of claiming to be a king. They knew that these two charges would have to be investigated by Pilate, whose primary responsibility as governor was to look out for the interests of Rome. According to all four Gospels, Pilate quickly concluded that these charges were not the real cause of their enmity toward Jesus (after all, since when were they interested in *Rome's* welfare?), and he sought to release him. Finally, however, he caved in under the threat of being accused himself of being disloyal to Caesar if he allowed a rival claimant to the throne to live: "If you release this man, you are not Caesar's friend. Everyone who makes himself a king opposes Caesar" (John 19.12). Pilate couldn't risk such a charge being brought against him, and although he recognized Jesus' innocence, he soon concluded that if it was his life or Jesus', then Jesus must die. "Then he handed him over to them to be crucified" (John 19.16).

Some question whether or not Pilate would have allowed himself to be bullied by the Jews in this way. After all, since he was the governor, they had no real power over him, and much of his history with them was one of oppression, not concession. But this is only partly true. Pilate despised the Jews over whom he ruled, and they returned the favor. (See, for example, the instance mentioned in Luke 13.1, about which nothing else is known.) He had blundered in his dealings with them almost from the day he arrived in Palestine; in spite of claims to the contrary, there is evidence that he could, indeed, be pressured by them into yielding to their will.

Shortly after his arrival in Palestine in AD 26, Pilate aroused the indignation of the Jews by bringing into Jerusalem Roman standards which bore images of the emperor, something abhorrent to Jewish sensibilities about "graven images." A delegation appealed to Pilate for five days to remove the standards, and on the sixth day Pilate ordered his soldiers to draw their swords. But the Jews bared their necks, ready to accept death rather than transgress their law. Fearing that a widespread revolt might result from killing so many over so sacred an issue, Pilate relented and removed the images from Jerusalem[3]. So there was historical precedent for forcing Pilate to give in, not because he wanted to please the Jews, but because he was unprincipled enough to sacrifice the life of one man in order to save himself a great deal of trouble. The Gospels in no way portray Pilate as a sympathetic figure; he was, rather, a man impaled on the horns of a dilemma, who took the safest way out for his own good and not because he cared anything about Jesus or his Jewish subjects.

So, historically speaking, why did Jesus die? The answer is multi-faceted. He died because he had aroused the resentment of the religious leaders of Judaism. He died because he claimed authority over some of the most sacred of Jewish institutions, including the Temple itself. He died because he predicted the eventual downfall of the Jewish system as it then existed. He died because some of his contemporaries (those who held religious power) considered him to be a blasphemer. He died because he was accused of insurrection, and because the Roman governor, who realized that Jesus was no political or military threat, was nonetheless too weak to resist the pressure to have him put to death. All of this is amply attested by the historical sources.

Are "the Jews" to Blame?

Before leaving the subject of why Jesus died, something needs to be said about the charge that the Gospels are "anti-Jewish"[4] in their depiction of his death. It is often charged that the New Testament generally (especially the Gospels) skews what actually happened in order to place the blame on the traditional enemies of Christianity, the Jews. One version of this says that Pilate and the Romans were actually to blame, with some suggesting that the Jewish authorities actually tried to save Jesus, but that Pilate was simply too blood-thirsty for them to be able to avert his death. Add to this the fact that hate groups have historically used the Gospels to show that the Jews are "Christ-killers" and ought to be subjected to all possible abuse. All of this taken together

---

[3] Josephus, *Jewish Wars* 2.9.2–3 and *Antiquities* 18.3.1

[4] The usual term is "anti-Semitic," but since many Jews regard the term "Semitic" as derogatory, I will use the less offensive term "anti-Jewish."

suggests that we need to look long and hard at the Gospels to see if this is what they actually say. Are they anti-Jewish?

First, it should be noted that just because the Gospels have been used to further anti-Jewish causes does not mean they are anti-Jewish in intent. It is true that the Gospels do not portray many Jews in a very positive light, because they deal primarily with the Jewish opponents of Jesus, but they never paint all Jews with the same brush, which would by definition be necessary in order to sustain the charge of anti-Judaism.

In fact, some Jews are presented in the Gospels in quite a positive light. All four Gospels mention that Joseph of Arimathea, who was not simply an ordinary Jew but a leader in the Jewish community and a member of the same council (the Sanhedrin) which condemned Jesus, courageously went to Pilate to ask for Jesus' body in order to bury it. This was a bold and benevolent move in light of what had just happened to Jesus and what could have happened to anyone who appeared to be friendly toward him (Matt 27.57–61; Mark 15.42–47; Luke 23.50–56; John 19.38–42). He was assisted in this task, John tells us, by Nicodemus, who is described as "a ruler of the Jews" and "*the* [not "a," as in some translations] teacher of Israel" and who had earlier challenged the Sanhedrin's readiness to condemn Jesus without a proper hearing (John 3.1, 10; 7.50–52).

It is true that the Gospel of John several times refers to the opponents of Jesus simply as "the Jews," which has occasioned the accusation that John intended to blame all Jews (including their descendants) for Jesus' death. However, it is usually overlooked that Josephus, the First-Century *Jewish* historian, uses exactly the same terminology to refer to those Zealots who defied Rome and thereby brought about the destruction of Jerusalem in AD 70. He blames the entire debacle on "the Jews," while obviously meaning only those who were responsible for leading the rebellion against Rome (*Wars* 2.466; 5.109–110; 6.71–79, 251–253). It is evident that John uses this term in the same way. Likewise, the Hebrew prophets of the Old Testament provide ample evidence of Jewish condemnation of unbelieving and rebellious Jews, so this is by no means unique to the Gospels, nor is it "anti-Jewish" in character (see, for only one of many examples, the entire book of Malachi).

Of special interest in this regard is Matthew 27.25, which reports that, after Pilate had "washed his hands" of Jesus, the people, under the influence of the chief priests and elders, cried out, "His blood be on us and on our children!"—the line that was famously left un-translated in the trial scene in Mel Gibson's *The Passion of the Christ*, although it was shouted in Aramaic by some in the crowd. This verse has been interpreted as meaning that all Jews for all time are collectively responsible for the death of Jesus. However, the "collective guilt" interpretation of this verse is entirely without merit. There is no record of God's ratifying the curse, nor does any New Testament writer suggest such a thing. Matthew simply reports that the people said it, and it should be left at that.

We must remember that the crucifixion of Jesus is the story of a Jew who was delivered for execution by Jews, as recorded by Jewish authors (with the exception of Luke, the lone Gentile writer in the New Testament). That means that the charge of "anti-Jewishness" makes very little sense at all, since both Jesus and his earliest followers were Jewish. The material in the Gospels that is negative toward Jews is in the specific context of those who opposed Jesus. To take it out of that context and use it against Jews today is to ignore both history and the legitimate interpretation of texts.

With all of this in mind, we must remember we are not dealing with a fantasy story that is subject to whatever interpretation we choose to put on it, based on our spiritual, nationalistic, or emotional inclinations. Rather, the death of Jesus is an event of history, one that is verified by both Jewish and non-Jewish sources from the First and Second Centuries, and we are not at liberty to re-write history, regardless of how distasteful we might personally find it. As someone has well said, to try to change history is to lose it, because if we have revised it to suit our personal tastes, the story of what actually happened will be lost. But the Jesus story is the story of the self-sacrificing love of Christ for the redemption of all humanity. It is not so much the story of "who killed Jesus" as of who Jesus is and why he died.

Yet the story includes that part about his enemies who insisted on his death and who actually executed him. There simply isn't any way to tell the story without that. To attempt to do so would be like trying to tell about the Holocaust without implicating any Germans. Including the account of what happened in no way condemns either group as a whole (and certainly not their descendants), nor does it provide any license for prejudice or hatred.

As a footnote, let me point out that the portrait of Jesus offered by some skeptics, such as those of the "Jesus Seminar," cannot possibly do justice to the historical fact of Jesus' death. Based largely on their anti-supernatural presuppositions and in an attempt to remove what they see as the "anti-Jewishness" of the Gospels, these critics strip the Gospels of all claims to the Deity, messiahship, and Lordship of Jesus. Instead, they present him as a wandering mystic who told nice stories and blessed little children, and never said anything to offend anyone. But by so doing, they make his death an enigma. Remember, the death of Jesus at the hands of Pilate and the insistence of the Jewish hierarchy is one of the most historically certain facts about him, attested by both Christian and non-Christian sources. But if he claimed nothing of what the Gospels say that he claimed for himself, we are left wondering: Why would anyone bother to kill him? The Jesus Seminar has much to explain.

Theological Reasons for Jesus' Death

We must acknowledge at the outset that these theological reasons for Jesus' death cannot be verified by history. Rather, they are matters of faith and can be neither proved nor disproved by historical means. But as we think about them, remember that the same sources which give us the historical reasons for Jesus' death give us these reasons as well. And, since we have seen that these sources are amply supported by external testimony, there is good reason to believe what they tell us theologically as well as historically. And, whether or not you choose to believe what the Gospels say about the theological reasons for Jesus' death, it is important at the least to acknowledge that this is what the early Christians believed about him. So, theologically speaking, why *did* Jesus die?

First, as I briefly mentioned earlier, Jesus himself said it was "necessary" that he die on the cross. What did he mean by that? When Jesus said in Luke 9.22 that "the Son of man must suffer many things, and be rejected by the elders and chief priests and scribes, and be killed, and on the third day be raised," he used a small Greek word (*dei*) that means "it is necessary," in the sense of a strong compulsion. It could be a divine compulsion (that is, the will of God), an inner compulsion, or what was required by the circumstances. In the case of Jesus, it was all of these and more, as we will see. It is important to note that to Jesus his impending death was no accident, nor was it something he sought to avoid. Rather, he viewed it as a divine necessity, one toward which his entire life was moving (see the other two "Passion Predictions," as they are called, in Luke 9.44 and 18.31–33). Remember that when he died he said, "It is finished!" (John 19.30). So what did he accomplish by his death? *What* was "finished"?

Matthew 26.26–28 is an important text in answering this question. As Jesus ate the Last Supper with his disciples, he took bread and wine and distributed it among them. The bread, he said, was his "body," and he referred to the cup as "my blood of the covenant, which is poured out for many for the forgiveness of sins." Two key ideas emerge here. One is that Jesus saw his death as instrumental in the establishment of a "new covenant" between God and his people. Just as the "Old Covenant" had been ratified through the shedding of the blood of animals, so now the New Covenant of Christ was to be brought about by the shedding of his own blood. (See also Heb 9.15–22 for a full discussion of this aspect of Jesus' blood and death.) But why? The other key idea in this text explains: "for the forgiveness of sins." When Jesus died, according to the New Testament, it was to provide a means of forgiveness. This is evidently why John 1.29 calls him "the Lamb of God, who takes away the sins of the world." Just as the Israelites sacrificed lambs and other animals in seeking atonement for their sins, so now Jesus offers his own blood (Hebrews 9 again) as the ultimate sacrifice for sins, one that never has to be repeated because it is entirely effective (see Heb 10.11–18; Rom 3.21–26).

The early Christians proclaimed as central to their message that "Christ died for our sins in accordance with the Scriptures" (1 Cor 15.3). Another way this is expressed in the New Testament is that Jesus bore our guilt and punishment for us. It is as if God had laid on him, as the sacrificial Lamb, all of the sins of the world, so that atonement might be made for them all. First Peter 2.24 expresses this eloquently, paraphrasing the words of Isaiah 53: "He himself bore our sins in his body on the tree, that we might die to sin and live to righteousness. By his wounds you have been healed."

I should point out here that it is impossible to make sense of the death of Jesus apart from the concept of *sin*. But sin is basically a foreign concept in today's world. That's why, for example, so many people came away from Mel Gibson's *The Passion of the Christ* saying, "I don't get it." They didn't "get it" because the film failed to make a strong enough connection between Jesus' sufferings and their purpose. Take sin out of the picture, and Jesus' death appears to be merely senseless brutality. Put it in, and we can all see our need for what Jesus did.

But even these lofty concepts cannot exhaust the meaning of the death of Jesus. Paul argues in Romans 5.12–21 that Jesus died in order to conquer death on our behalf. By embracing death for us and then rising from the dead, Jesus won the victory in which we are all invited to share. This means, according to Hebrews 2.14–15, that we have not only been set free from death but also from the fear of it. Someone has said that death is "the worm at the core of all of our pretensions to happiness." Whether that gloomy assessment is entirely correct or not, the New Testament joyfully proclaims that, through Jesus, we don't have to be afraid any more.

The apostle Paul sees the death of Jesus as, among other things, setting us free from what he calls "the curse of the law" (Gal 3.13–14). This does not mean that Paul sees the Old Testament law itself as a curse. Rather, "the curse of the law" is our inability to keep it and the condemnation which results from that failure. A system of laws could save us only if we were capable of keeping them all perfectly (Jas 2.10–11); otherwise, the laws themselves stand in judgment against us. Laws can help deter wrongdoing, but they cannot amend it once broken; rather, they stand as our judges. But, Paul says, by his death on the cross, Jesus has done something for us that the Law, "weakened by the flesh, could not do. By sending his own Son in the likeness of sinful flesh and for sin, he condemned sin in the flesh…" (Rom 8.3). So, through Jesus' death for us, we are free from the "curse of the law," the fact that we are incapable of pleasing God by our own power. Now we can be free through faith in Jesus' blood.

Closely connected to this freedom from the Law is the concept of having "died to sin" and become "alive to righteousness" through Jesus' own death. In Romans 6.1–4 Paul responds to the question of whether or not the grace of God bestowed through Jesus means we can "sin all the more that grace may abound." His reply: "By no means!" (King James Version: "God forbid!") Why not? "Do you not know that all of us who have been baptized into Christ Jesus were baptized into his death? We were buried therefore with him by baptism into death, in order that, just as Christ was raised from the dead by the glory of the Father, we too might walk in newness of life." Not only did Jesus die *for* us, Paul says, but through baptism we can participate in his death, in anticipation of also being raised with him from the dead. Hebrews 9.11–14 conveys a similar thought by saying that by his death Jesus

> …entered once for all into the holy places (the 'Holy of Holies' in the Temple, where no one but the high priest was ever allowed to go, and he but once a year), not by means of the blood of goats and calves but by means of his own blood, thus securing an eternal redemption. For if the sprinkling of defiled persons with the blood of goats and bulls and with the ashes of a heifer sanctifies for the purification of the flesh, how much more will the blood of Christ, who through the eternal Spirit offered himself without blemish to God, purify our conscience from dead works to serve the living God.

One more reason Jesus died was to set an example for us of suffering unjustly while doing right. It is simply a fact of life that people often suffer, not because they have done something wrong, but because they have insisted on doing what is right. While, according to the New Testament, this is not the primary reason for Jesus' death, it served as a powerful example for his followers who soon encountered the opposition of an unbelieving world, and it continues to do so today. So Peter writes,

> For this is a gracious thing, when, mindful of God, one endures sorrows while suffering unjustly. For what credit is it if, when you sin and are beaten for it, you endure? But if when you do good and suffer for it you endure, this is a gracious thing in the sight of God. For to this you have been called, because Christ also suffered for you, leaving you an example, so that you might follow in his steps. He committed no sin; neither was deceit found in his mouth. When he was reviled, he did not revile in return; when he suffered, he did not threaten; but continued entrusting himself to him who judges justly. He himself bore our sins in his body on the tree, that we might die to sin and live to righteousness. By his wounds you have been healed. (1 Pet 2.21–24)

There are still more ways in which the New Testament expresses theologically the reason for Jesus' death. But these are enough to help you see the general trend of early Christian thinking. And remember, these are not simply the random ideas of believers as they reflected on what Jesus had done and why he died. They all have their roots in his own words: "…for this is my blood of the covenant, which is poured out for many, for the forgiveness of sins." And they help us understand the multi-faceted nature of the death of Jesus. His was not simply an execution, the tragic ending of a confused religious zealot. Rather, it was the carefully planned sacrifice of one who gave his life as a ransom for many.

Additional Note: Judas – Why Did He Do It?

Betrayal of a friend is an act that is always looked on with scorn; this is especially the case with Judas' betrayal of Jesus. It raises the troubling question of why anyone would do such a thing, especially one of Jesus' own followers. Numerous suggestions have been offered:

He wasn't really a disciple. The assumption here is that Judas had been faking it all along, but nothing in the New Testament suggests that Jesus regarded him that way, although the Gospel of John says that Jesus knew who was going to betray him. But remember that all of The Twelve had their shortcomings, and this didn't mean they weren't "real disciples." Besides, Acts 1.15–20 indicates that Judas had a legitimate place among The Twelve, and Jesus washed the feet of Judas, just as he did the others, at the Last Supper, even though he knew what he was going to do (John 13.1–30).

Greed. It is widely known that Judas betrayed Jesus for "thirty pieces of silver" (Matt 26.14–15; 27.3), and the Gospel of John states that Judas was a thief and was in charge of the "money box" for the group of disciples who traveled with Jesus (John 12.6; 13.29). However, 30 pieces of silver was not a particularly large sum of money; so, while greed may have played a role, it does not seem likely to have been Judas' primary motive. We have to look a little deeper.

Fear. We know from the Gospels that Peter denied Jesus out of fear for his life, and it may be that Judas betrayed him for the same reason. It certainly was a dangerous thing to be associated with someone who seemed determined to be at odds with the authorities and who had often predicted his own death.

Conviction. Positively, it has been suggested that Judas may have betrayed Jesus in order to "jump start" a revolt.

This would mean that Judas was a true believer in Jesus' messiahship and that he felt he needed to help the process along by turning Jesus over to his enemies with the expectation that Jesus would then lead the messianic revolt many Jews longed for. This would explain his remorse when he saw things weren't going to go in that direction (Matt 27.3–10). Negatively, Judas may have initially been convinced of Jesus' messiahship until their arrival in Jerusalem, but when he saw that Jesus really was going to get himself killed, as predicted, decided not to go down with a sinking ship, concluding that Jesus must not be the Messiah anyway.

Whatever his motives, Judas will forever be remembered as "the one who betrayed him," the way the writers of the Gospels almost always speak of him.

Think About It

1. Explain why crucifixion was such an important tool for the Romans in keeping control throughout the Empire.

2. Why was Jesus' death by crucifixion problematic for the early church? How did they deal with this problem?

3. What mental images does the word "cross" bring to your mind? How does this compare with what the word "cross" meant to people in the First-Century Roman Empire?

4. In what way was Jesus' death the result of a complex set of circumstances involving both Roman and Jewish authorities?

5. Do you think it was appropriate that Matthew 27.25 was omitted (in translation, at least) from the scene of Jesus' trial in Mel Gibson's "The Passion of the Christ"? Why or why not?

6. Someone has said that to change history is to lose it. What do you think of this statement? How does it affect the way the Gospels tell the story of Jesus?

7. Why is the concept of sin so important in understanding why Jesus died? What happens when this concept is removed from the total picture?

7

Did Jesus Really Rise from the Dead?

Impossible?

Probably no aspect of Jesus' life and death is more controversial than the New Testament claim that, after his crucifixion at the hands of the Romans, he arose bodily from the dead. After all, this is completely beyond the realm of normal human experience, and all of our dealings with death tell us that people don't recover from it—period. Yes, there are people who claim to have died and then returned, but these are highly subjective experiences beyond the realm of verification. Also, even if these people actually died and came back to life, they are not expected to continue to live forever, as the New Testament claims for Jesus. So their experiences, even if real, are not truly parallel. Ironically, many people are more ready to believe these anecdotal reports than to believe in the possibility of Jesus' resurrection based on the documents which report it.

The first thought of many when confronted with the idea of Jesus' resurrection is "That's impossible!" Usually that ends their thinking on the subject, since modern science knows of no such possibility. However, we should be cautious about flatly stating that something is impossible—especially something involving the divine. In fact, the only way to declare that something such as Jesus' resurrection is "impossible" is to rule God out of the picture entirely, which, of course, some do. But as long as we admit even the *possibility* of God's existence (and, philosophically speaking, we must admit it since it can't be disproved), then we cannot say that Jesus' resurrection is "impossible." So, unless you're a hardened skeptic about the existence of God, you should be willing to grant the possibility of resurrection and go a step further in your thinking. That next step is, as we maintained earlier, to ask not about *possibility* but about *probability*. Remember that this is the historian's task: to reconstruct from the evidence what is most probable about events of the past. So that's what we need to ask about Jesus' resurrection: What is the probability that he rose from the dead?

What's at Stake?
Before proceeding to that part of the discussion, we should pause to ask, "What is really at stake in this question?" How important is it to answer it? Why can't we just discuss what we can know about Jesus' life and death and leave off any consideration of the controversial subject of his resurrection? Wouldn't we be on safer ground, both historically and spiritually, to simply avoid discussing the resurrection and let each person think what he or she chooses about it? These are all good questions, and they deserve to be addressed.

When I was in graduate school, I was required in a doctoral seminar to read a scholarly article by an acclaimed German theologian on the subject of the historicity (i.e., whether or not it happened) of the resurrection. The author spent over 30 pages discussing the pros and cons of this important question, then reached the conclusion that in the final analysis it really doesn't matter whether Jesus rose from the dead or not. What is important, he said, is that on Easter morning the believer can "have the resurrection glow in his heart," whether or not the event actually happened. I was stunned. How could anyone who was even *trying* to think historically say that something like Jesus' resurrection from the dead "doesn't matter"? How could this brilliant thinker make the sudden shift from valid historical inquiry to subjective religious experience without batting an eye?

Remember our opening comments about Neil Armstrong's moon walk? He either did or he didn't. We can't say that what really matters is whether or not we have "the moon-walk glow" in our imaginations. It's the same with Jesus' resurrection. He either did or he didn't. That makes the resurrection a valid subject of historical inquiry, especially since we have multiple sources which say he did rise. This isn't to say that in the final analysis we can "prove" or "disprove" the resurrection, but we can certainly discuss the question of probability. It won't do simply to dismiss the whole subject with the wave of a hand (or pen) and say that "it doesn't matter." If Jesus *did* rise from the dead, then we would be dismissing as irrelevant the most significant moment in human history. Intellectual honesty forbids us to do that. And why should we want to? Non-believers should welcome the opportunity to de-bunk such a fantastic myth. Believers should welcome the opportunity to substantiate it.

The writers of the New Testament were completely aware of the high-stakes nature of this question, as their comments clearly reveal. They knew the resurrection was a make-it-or-break-it concept as far as the Christian faith was concerned. Paul even went so far as to declare that removing the resurrection invalidates the Christian message entirely! In 1 Corinthians 15.3–5 he lists the death, burial, resurrection, and post-resurrection appearances of Jesus as the things "of first importance" that he had preached to the Corinthians. Then in verses 12–19 he argues "if Christ has not been raised, then our preaching is in vain and your faith is in vain… If Christ has not been raised, your faith is futile and you are still in your sins. Then those also who have fallen asleep in Christ have perished." Notice that Paul does not shy away from the implications of his preaching but says without hesitation that the whole thing (the gospel) stands or falls on the reality of the resurrection. (I wonder what *he* would have thought of that theologian's article.)

But why? Why can't there be a resurrection-less Christianity? After all, it would still honor Jesus and teach a good way to live. But those things aren't the issue as far as Paul is concerned. In Romans 1.1–4 he gives a remarkable summary of the gospel which he preached. In doing so he calls it "the gospel…concerning [God's] Son, who was descended from David according to the flesh and was declared to be the Son of God in power according to the Spirit of holiness by his resurrection from the dead, Jesus Christ our Lord…."

What does Paul mean when he says Jesus was "*declared to be* the Son of God…by his resurrection"? Some have understood this to mean that Jesus *became* God's Son when he was raised from the dead, but this isn't Paul's point. The resurrection didn't *make* Jesus the Son of God. According to Paul, it "showed him to be" God's Son. It was a demonstration that Jesus was, in fact, who he claimed to be (see ch 5). Paul knew this in a very personal way, because it was seeing Jesus risen from the dead that convinced him that Jesus must truly be the Messiah of Israel rather than the impostor Paul had at first believed him to be (Acts 9.1–5; 1 Cor 9.1).

Paul isn't the only one who understands Jesus' resurrection in this way. Acts 2.14–36 contains a synopsis of what may rightly be called "the first Christian sermon," in that it was the first time Jesus' identity was proclaimed following the cross and resurrection. Peter is the speaker, and after declaring that the phenomena witnessed by the crowd of Jews gathered in Jerusalem for Pentecost (vv 1–13) were the fulfillment of the messianic prophecy of Joel 2.28–34, he begins to discuss Jesus in verse 22. Notice how quickly Peter moves from the events of Jesus' life and death (vv 22–23) to his resurrection, which is clearly the centerpiece of his sermon. He argues, based on a prophetic text from Psalms 16 that *someone* was to be raised from the dead: "For you will not abandon my soul to Hades nor let your Holy One see corruption" (v 27). He then argues that David couldn't have been talking about himself, since it was common knowledge that David had died and was buried and the location of his tomb was still known. He goes on to state that David was *not* talking about himself but about "the resurrection of the Christ (Messiah)" (v 31) and concludes, "Let all the house of Israel therefore know for certain that God has made him both Lord and Christ, this Jesus whom you crucified" (v 36). The resurrection pointed to Jesus' identity as Lord and Christ (Messiah). Without it, he was simply one more messianic pretender.

So, as far as the New Testament is concerned, there is a great deal at stake in the question of whether or not Jesus actually rose from the dead: the very validity of the Christian faith. And it is more than a bit ironic that so many professed Christians today fail to grasp this aspect of the gospel.

So Where's the Evidence?

Now that we have a clear picture of what's at stake in the discussion about Jesus' resurrection, let's go back to the probability question. Is there any evidence that would suggest that Jesus probably rose from the dead? Let's see.[1]

First, there is the testimony of the ancient sources. The earliest sources on this subject are the New Testament writings themselves. And the remarkable thing here is that all of the ancient texts say (or assume) the same thing: Jesus rose from the dead. All four New Testament Gospels report Jesus as having been raised, and the early preaching of the apostles recorded in Acts claims the same, as does Paul (1 Cor 15; Rom 1.1–4; etc.). Paul's statements are of special importance, having been written some 20 to 25 years earlier than the Gospels (by most estimates, depending on conclusions regarding the dating of the Gospels). Paul's statement in 1 Corinthians 15 that if Christ has not been raised the Christian faith is invalid was written in the mid-50s AD. Even earlier is his statement in 1 Thessalonians 4.14: "For since we believe that Jesus died and rose again, even so, through Jesus, God will bring with him those who have fallen asleep," written most likely in AD 51–52. It is one thing to argue that by the time the Gospels were written, perhaps 40 or more years after the fact, a "resurrection myth" had arisen in the early church. This would be a strikingly short time for the formulation and acceptance of such a myth, but it is quite another thing to say that this had happened by the time that Paul wrote, only about *20* years after the fact. Given that short span of time, there still would have been people alive who

---

[1]See also the discussion of these points in Gary L. Habermas, "Why I Believe the Miracles of Jesus Actually Happened," in *Why I Am a Christian: Leading Thinkers Explain Why They Believe*, rev. and exp. edition, eds. N. L. Geisler and P. K. Hoffman (Baker, 2006), 126–134.

could have argued to the contrary, that Jesus was not raised, that his dead body had been seen after the supposed resurrection, etc. Paul even goes so far as to tell of a post-resurrection appearance to "more than five hundred brothers at one time, most of whom are still alive, though some have fallen asleep" (1 Cor 15.6). It's as if Paul were saying, "There are eyewitnesses still around; go ahead, ask them!" That's quite a bold claim if Paul knew it wasn't true.

The bottom line is, all of the most ancient sources say Jesus rose from the dead. There are none that say he did not. If it were acceptable to have a resurrection-less Christianity, surely one or more of the New Testament writers would have reflected this.[2]

Second, there is the fact of Jesus' burial. That Jesus was buried following his crucifixion may not seem all that significant to us, but it was to the authors of the New Testament. All four Gospels report the burial of Jesus (Matt 27.57–61; Mark 15.42–47; Luke 23.50–56; John 19.38–42). All of these accounts are in accord with Jewish burial customs as we can determine them from other ancient sources. Corpses were normally prepared for burial by being washed, anointed with spices (for odor control as much as honor), and wrapped in shrouds. Mark 16.1 and Luke 24.1 report that the women who went to the tomb very early on that Sunday morning did so in order to anoint Jesus' body with spices. Remember that Jesus had been buried in haste, since the Sabbath was approaching, so there was not time for a proper burial (John 19.41–42). Niches hewn in the walls of caves and closed with large stones were often used for burials, and there are many of these in Palestine, dating from the time of Jesus. So the Gospels are consistent with one another in reporting the burial of Jesus, and what they say about it is consistent with what we know from other sources as well.

The fact that we have so much information from the Gospels concerning Jesus' burial suggests the importance of this aspect of the story of Jesus for these writers. Likewise, Paul lists the fact that Jesus "was buried" as one of the things "of first importance"

---

[2] "There is no form of early Christianity known to us—though there are some that have been invented by ingenious scholars—that does not affirm at its heart that after Jesus' shameful death God raised him to life again" (N. T. Wright, *The Challenge of Jesus: Rediscovering Who Jesus Was and Is* [InterVarsity, 1999], 126).

in the gospel message he proclaimed (1 Cor 15.4). So why is the burial of Jesus so important, and how does it serve as evidence regarding the resurrection?

The significance isn't so hard to see. Jesus' burial authenticates his death and is the necessary prelude to the resurrection. If Jesus was physically dead, it helps us understand what the New Testament means by his "resurrection." In other words, it was not merely a "spiritual" resurrection (whatever that means), as often suggested, but the resurrection of his previously dead body. It is almost as if the ancient writers were attempting to answer in advance some of the common objections that have been raised to the resurrection: He wasn't really dead, only passed out and later revived in the tomb. Or he "arose," but not physically; rather, he "came alive again" in the hearts of his followers. But the Gospels want us to know that Jesus was fully and physically dead. If there had been a doctor present, armed with all the instruments of modern medical analysis, he would have pronounced Jesus dead: no pulse, no brain-wave activity, no respiration—dead. And, being dead, he was buried. And this sets the stage for his resurrection.

And, if Jesus was buried, then something had to have happened to his body. How easy it would have been for the Jewish authorities—or Pilate—to have produced the dead body if it had remained in the tomb and in this manner squashed the new Christian movement before it even began! Amazingly, they didn't—couldn't. But this leads to our next point.

Third, there is the matter of the empty tomb. When the women went to the tomb on Sunday morning, they found it empty. Somehow that must be explained. Did they go to the wrong tomb, one that had not yet been used? Not likely, since Mark 15.47 adds this note to the account of Jesus' burial: "Mary Magdalene and Mary the mother of Joses saw where he was laid." Luke 23.55 further adds, "The women who had come with him from Galilee followed, and saw the tomb, and how his body was laid." Both Mark and Luke seem determined to head off the supposition that the women got lost in the dim light of the early morning and went to the wrong grave.

Some explanation must be offered for the emptiness of Jesus' tomb. That's only logical, isn't it? If it were to be discovered that John F. Kennedy's grave in Arlington National Cemetery is actually empty, do you suppose there would be no inquiries into the whereabouts of the body? Every possibility would be explored in order to explain what happened to it. It would have to be somewhere. Well, it's no different with the body of Jesus. If it wasn't in the tomb, then where was it?

In opposing the idea of the resurrection, some point out that in their preaching about the resurrection the apostles didn't make a big deal of the empty tomb, as if to say that this is more of a modern invention than an ancient reality and thus not a very convincing argument. But this is only partially true. Consider Peter's sermon on Pentecost (Acts 2.22–36). When Peter made the point, based on Psalms 16, that God's "holy one" would not see corruption or his body see decay, he didn't hesitate to claim, "Brothers, I may say to you with confidence about the patriarch David that he both died and was buried, and his tomb is with us to this day" (Acts 2.29). While Peter didn't specifically mention the empty tomb of Jesus, the implication is clear enough: Jesus' tomb is empty; David's isn't. Besides, one reason for not mentioning the empty tomb more in the apostles' preaching is the fact that the apostles were eyewitnesses of the risen Christ. Naturally, the empty tomb would take a back seat to that as a line of evidence. But for us today there must be *some* explanation of why the tomb was found empty.

Attempts to discard the reality of the empty tomb and its significance have ranged from the fanciful to the comical, but none have ever won a very wide following, even among scholars who are of a skeptical nature. The suggestion that Jesus' enemies stole his body in order to prevent a trumped-up resurrection claim is simply illogical: The last thing they would want is a tomb with no body in it. Alternatively, the idea that Jesus' own followers stole his body to make it look as if he had risen is equally implausible, since they eventually died for their claim. Such ideas as the "swoon theory" (Jesus wasn't really dead and revived in the cool of the tomb, then exited on his own) hardly deserve serious consideration and don't usually get any.

More recently, John Dominic Crossan, of Jesus Seminar fame, has taken a different approach by arguing that Jesus' body was never buried at all. Operating entirely from speculation, Crossan says Jesus' enemies could not have been expected to give his body a decent burial, and his friends wouldn't have been allowed to do so, so it was most likely cast into a shallow grave by his executioners, then eaten by dogs.[3] He dismisses the Gospels' claim that Joseph of Arimathea, who was a respected member of the Jewish council (Sanhedrin), requested Jesus' body from Pilate and saw to the burial, simply by claiming (again without historical evidence) that it didn't happen. Rather, he claims, "If they had power, they were not his friends; if they were his friends, they had no power."[4] It is simply not good historical methodology to make such rash claims without supporting evidence from the sources. Crossan's efforts to deny that Jesus' body was ever buried must be seen as what they are: desperate measures to avoid having to explain the empty tomb.

Fourth, there is the manner in which the resurrection is reported. One of the standard critical arguments against the reality of the resurrection is that the early church invented it (some say Paul did) to try to give validity to their new religion. The idea is that Jesus didn't claim to be the Messiah, Son of God, etc., nor did he actually work miracles, and he certainly did not rise from the dead. So, in essence, the argument is that the writers of the Gospels made up a fictitious narrative (or four separate ones, since they don't agree in every detail) to the effect that Jesus rose from the dead and is still alive. This all sounds logical, but there are some serious flaws in the reasoning.

For one thing, it is problematic, if Matthew, Mark, Luke, and John merely invented the resurrection story, that they didn't record anyone actually *seeing* the event itself. The Gospels report that Jesus died and was buried, but that when the women came

---

[3]John Dominic Crossan, *Jesus: A Revolutionary Biography* (HarperSanFrancisco, 1995), 154.

[4]John Dominic Crossan, *The Historical Jesus: The Life of a Mediterranean Jewish Peasant* (HarperSanFrancisco, 1991), 393.

on Sunday they found the tomb empty. There were no witnesses of Jesus' emerging from the tomb, only of the empty tomb and, later, of the risen Christ. (Matthew 28.11 may suggest that the soldiers guarding the grave saw Jesus exit, but it is unclear if "all that had taken place" necessarily includes this.) Now, this is a rather peculiar—and unconvincing—way to invent a resurrection myth, don't you think? If the story were merely invented, one would expect the four Evangelists (as the Gospel writers are often called) to have provided some pretty impressive witnesses. Surely the Jewish high priest would have been there, or perhaps even Pilate, all verifying that Jesus had truly risen from the dead and unable to deny that they had seen it. The fact that our four authors don't "bulk up" the witness list argues for their truthfulness. In other words, they don't try to tell more than they actually know.

Another point to consider: The first to see the empty tomb and the risen Christ were women. That's not so startling in our day, but in First-Century Judaism it would be like having no witnesses at all. Women did not give testimony in court, and were generally considered to be unreliable witnesses for much of anything. The New Testament reflects this in reporting the resurrection of Jesus. Luke plainly states that when the women went to the disciples to tell them what they had found, "these words seemed to them an idle tale, and they did not believe them" (24.11). Also, the Gospels are very candid about the slowness to believe exhibited by Jesus' male followers. Matthew 28.17 says that when the disciples met Jesus on the mountain in Galilee to which he had directed them, "when they saw him they worshiped him, but some doubted." And John records the famous story of Thomas, who upon hearing that Jesus had been raised and had appeared to the other disciples said, "Unless I see in his hands the mark of the nails, and place my finger into the mark of the nails, and place my hand into his side, I will never believe" (20.25). Odd, isn't it, that writers who were trying to convince unbelievers that the resurrection was true would report that even those closest to Jesus didn't believe at first? And that they were themselves in the category of unreliable witnesses? Not very convincing story-telling!

One would think that Matthew, Mark, Luke, and John wouldn't have included these potentially embarrassing details unless they knew—or at least believed—them to be true.

Fifth, there are the post-resurrection appearances. It is important to note that when Paul sets forth the things of "first importance" for the church at Corinth, he includes, along with the death, burial, and resurrection, that Jesus made numerous appearances to his followers after being raised (1 Cor 1.5–8; see also Acts 1.3, which says these appearances took place over a period of 40 days). These include not only appearances to the 11 disciples, but also to "more than five hundred brothers at one time," to James (probably Jesus' own brother—see below), and finally to Paul himself. Some, but obviously not all, of these appearances are recorded in the four Gospels and in the accounts of Paul's own conversion and calling to apostleship in Acts 9, 22, and 26.

We have already noted that the Gospels report in all honesty that his own followers were slow to believe. The post-resurrection appearances were therefore necessary to convince even Jesus' own disciples that he had actually risen from the dead and to qualify them as eyewitnesses of the resurrection, which later would become their primary function. The fact that there were so many appearances to such a variety of people and that Paul practically invites interviews with some of the witnesses, argues for their historicity. Otherwise, why mention them at all, if they would have been unconvincing?

Sixth, there are the conversions of Saul and James. No one was more skeptical of the truth of Jesus' identity and resurrection than Saul of Tarsus, later to be known as the apostle Paul. He was at first a persecutor of the Christian movement (see Acts 9; 22; 26; Gal 1.13–14; 1 Tim 1.12–15). Acts presents him as a sort of "public enemy number one" as far as the church was concerned, and reports that, following his conversion, the church enjoyed a time of unprecedented peace (9.31). Likewise, Paul mentions that Jesus had appeared "to James" (1 Cor 15.7). Since he mentions an appearance "to the twelve" prior to this (v 5) and "to all the apostles" (v 7), it appears that this is a James who was not an apostle. Who might this James be, and why does Paul regard this appearance as being so significant?

The most probable explanation is that this is James the brother of Jesus, who became a leader in the early church and is the most likely author of the New Testament letter of James. Like Paul, James probably became a believer as a result of such an appearance. Mark 3.21 reports that at one point Jesus' family "went out to seize him, for people were saying, 'He is out of his mind.'" In other words, people in Jesus' home area thought his words and actions were crazy, and the family came out to take charge of him. No wonder that later, when it was reported to Jesus that "Your mother and your brothers are outside, asking for you," he responded, "Whoever does the will of God is my brother, and sister, and mother" (Mark 3.31–35). John 7.5 states flatly that "even his brothers did not believe in him." Yet Acts 1.14 says that following Jesus' resurrection and ascension back into heaven, the remaining eleven apostles "with one accord were devoting themselves to prayer, together with the women and Mary the mother of Jesus, *and his brothers.*" Apparently, sometime between the crucifixion and Acts 1, James had become a believer. A post-resurrection appearance would certainly account for this in James' case, as in Paul's, and perhaps is the most satisfactory explanation, given that both men had been adamantly unconvinced at an earlier time.

Seventh, there is the willingness of the disciples to die for proclaiming the resurrection. This one is patently obvious. According to early Christian traditions, Jesus' original 12 apostles (except for John and, of course, Judas) were martyred for their testimony that Jesus had been crucified and had risen from the dead. It is difficult to explain their willingness to face death for something they knew to be a hoax, if in fact they knew that Jesus had not actually risen from the dead. Surely at least one of them would have cracked and exposed the whole business as a sham. There is no historical evidence that even one of them did so.

Eighth, there is the existence of the church. No one can deny on historical grounds that the early church sprang into existence suddenly and spread rapidly following the death of Jesus. And, of course, it continues to this day. Something must be proposed historically to account for this phenomenon, especially in view of the fact that the early followers of Jesus were so often persecuted and killed, and some still are. Of course, many movements have begun and thrived under persecution. What makes Christianity unique is the suddenness with which it came on the scene and the speed with which it spread. The firm conviction that Jesus had risen from the dead, and that he offered hope for life everlasting to those who followed him, would explain these phenomena. It is difficult to imagine anything else that would. James D. G. Dunn has recently argued that the Christian movement can only be explained adequately on the basis of the impact Jesus made on his first followers, and that the Gospels are the result of the impression that he made on them. "The historical fact of Christianity is impossible to explain without the historical fact of Jesus of Nazareth and of the impression he left." [5] That "impression" resulted in the Gospel accounts of his resurrection. Ben Witherington III concurs with this judgment:

> In other words, I am claiming that after the crucifixion, it took a miracle to generate the church—indeed, even to generate the inner circle of Jesus' followers. Our earliest sources, by their own confession, are clear that almost the entire inner circle of male disciples denied, deserted, or betrayed Jesus, while the women watched him die and then went to lay a wreath, as it were, on the tomb. It is the historical event we call Easter that reversed this drastic trend, without which the story of Jesus would have been left in the dustbin of history. [6]

He's Still Alive?

A corollary to the New Testament claim that Jesus rose from the dead is that he is still alive. From the perspective of Christian faith, this is an important part of the entire picture. Let's hear what Paul has to say:

---

[5] James D. G. Dunn, *A New Perspective on Jesus: What the Quest for the Historical Jesus Missed* (Baker Academic, 2005), 22–23.

[6] Ben Witherington III, *What Have They Done With Jesus?* (HarperOne, 2007), 11.

But in fact Christ has been raised from the dead, the firstfruits of those who have fallen asleep. For as by a man came death, by a man has come also the resurrection of the dead. For as in Adam all die, so also in Christ shall all be made alive. But each in his own order: Christ the firstfruits, then at his coming those who belong to Christ. Then comes the end, when he delivers the kingdom to God the Father after destroying every rule and every authority and power. For he must reign until he has put all his enemies under his feet. The last enemy to be destroyed is death. (1 Cor 15.20–26)

It is the fact of Jesus' continuing life that offers hope for the ultimate future of believers, when even death itself will cease to be a problem.

Likewise, Hebrews 7.23–25, after arguing that Jesus is the ultimate "high priest" and superior to the priests who served under Moses, asserts,

The former priests were many in number, because they were prevented by death from continuing in office, but he holds his priesthood permanently, because he continues forever. Consequently, he is able for all time to save to the uttermost those who draw near to God through him, since he always lives to make intercession for them.

Believers in Jesus' death and resurrection find great comfort in the fact that he not only died but is now alive forever and can thus be of help and provide spiritual intercession with God for those who follow him.

So there's a lot riding on our question: Did Jesus really rise from the dead? Look at the evidence, and decide for yourself.

Additional Note 1: Jewish Burial Customs

• Burial of the dead was regarded as a religious duty. To be left unburied was the ultimate shame and dishonor. This would explain why a devout Pharisee such as Joseph of Arimathea would run the risk of asking for Jesus' body in order to bury it.

• Corpses were not embalmed but were prepared for burial by being washed, anointed with oils and spices, and wrapped in shrouds. The Gospels specify the latter two as part of Jesus' burial.

• Candles were lit at the head and feet of the corpse. This was probably not done in Jesus' case, since burial was done quickly because of the approaching Sabbath.

• Burial occurred before dark on the day of death if possible.

• Professional mourners were often part of funerals. See Mark 5.38–39.

• Niches hewn out of the walls of caves were common burial sites. There are numerous examples of burial caves closed by large stones as in the tombs of Lazarus and Jesus (John 11.38; Mark 16.3–4). Wooden coffins or stone sarcophagi were sometimes used.

• It was believed by many that the spirit remained near the dead body for three days, then departed.

• Around the time of Jesus, secondary burials often occurred. The bones would be exhumed, placed in a small stone box called an ossuary, and reburied. In April, 2002, an ossuary bearing the inscription "James Son of Joseph brother of Jesus" surfaced from an Israeli collector. If the "James" mentioned is the brother of Jesus of Nazareth, this would be the first archaeological link relating directly to

Jesus and his family. However, its authenticity is widely disputed, and it would be impossible to prove beyond doubt that it does relate to Jesus, since all three names in the inscription were quite common. (Adapted from Everett Ferguson, *Backgrounds of Early Christianity*, Third Edition [Eerdmans, 2003], 244–246.)

Additional Note 2: The Post-Resurrection Appearances in the New Testament

"To them he presented himself alive after his suffering by many proofs, appearing to them during forty days and speaking about the kingdom of God" (Acts 1.3).

Matthew 28.9–10. To the two Mary's at the tomb. Jesus tells them that his disciples will see him in Galilee.

Matthew 28.16–20. To the eleven disciples on a mountain in Galilee. Jesus tells them, "Go and make disciples of all nations."

Mark 16.9–20. To Mary Magdalene, two unnamed disciples, and the eleven. Note: This text does not occur in the most ancient manuscripts of Mark and does not appear to have originally been a part of the Gospel. It seems to be a combining of elements of appearances mentioned in the other Gospels. If this is correct, then Mark originally recorded no post-resurrection appearance, only the announcement by a "young man" (angel) about Jesus' being raised.

Luke 24.13–35. To two disciples, one named Cleopas and the other unnamed, on the road to the village of Emmaus. Jesus eats with them and explains the Old Testament Scriptures concerning himself.

Luke 24.36–53. To the eleven in Jerusalem. Jesus demonstrates his physical reality, opens their minds to understand the Scriptures concerning himself, and commissions them to wait in Jerusalem until the coming of "power from on high."

John 20.11–18. To Mary Magdalene, outside the tomb. She at first mistakes him for the gardener but then recognizes him. He tells her of his impending ascension into heaven.

John 20.19–23. To ten of the disciples. He shows them his hands and side and commissions them to proclaim the forgiveness of sins.

John 20.26–29. To the eleven. Thomas, who was not present at the previous appearance, becomes convinced that it is indeed Jesus.

John 21.1–23. To the eleven, beside the Sea of Galilee. Jesus questions, then commissions, Peter. (Note: This chapter is believed by some scholars to be a later addition to John's Gospel, but even if this is correct, it may still record an actual appearance.)

Acts 1.1–11. To the eleven. Jesus promises the Holy Spirit's coming and commissions them to be his witnesses "to the end of the earth."

Acts 9, 22 , 26. Three accounts of Jesus' appearance to Saul (later Paul) on the road to Damascus, resulting in his conversion and calling to apostleship.

1 Corinthians 15.5–8. Paul summarizes several accounts, some of which are not recorded elsewhere in the New Testament (those to the "five hundred" and to James).

Think About It

1. What aspects of the Christian faith would be changed if the resurrection of Jesus were removed as an actual event of history?

2. Why was Jesus' burial an inherent part of the early Christian preaching about him? Do you think this concept receives much emphasis today? If not, why not?

3. Why do you think that many people find the idea of Jesus' resurrection difficult to believe?

4. Given complete license to write the most convincing story possible regardless of the facts, how might Matthew, Mark, Luke, and John have written their accounts of the resurrection in a more convincing way? What details might they have included or omitted?

5. The Gospels do not agree in every detail in reporting Jesus' resurrection. What might account for this? Is this a positive or a negative as far as making them believable?

8

Is It Possible to Know Jesus Today?

Sometimes in reading a biographical sketch of a person, one of the categories of information will be something like "Person from history I'd most like to meet." And it isn't unusual for that person (or one of them, if there's a short list) to be "Jesus of Nazareth." From all the remarkable things the Bible and other histories tell us about Jesus, he's certainly someone whom most of us would like to meet.

I'm sure you understand that there is a difference between *knowing about* someone and actually *knowing* that person. In studying history we can learn a great deal about people of the past, but that doesn't mean we know them. So far in this book, as its title indicates, we've focused on what we can know *about* Jesus. We've asked the kinds of historical questions about him that we might ask about any other important figure of history, such as our sources of information about him; when, where, and how he lived; what language(s) he spoke; what he thought about himself; what he believed; how he died; and whether or not it's possible that he actually rose from the dead.

Now we come to a question that the writers of the New Testament (who are our primary sources of information about Jesus) urge us to ask: Is it possible to know Jesus today? While not strictly a historical question, it arises because of what Jesus' history tells us—especially the fact that he died but rose again and therefore is still alive. And, if there's any truth to that, then it opens the possibility that we can actually know him. Not just "about" him, but him. I realize we're getting into the realms of theology and personal belief here, things that can't be conclusively demonstrated through the usual channels of historical study. But if what we have learned about Jesus has any validity at all, then this is a question that we have to ask. And the sources which tell us *about* Jesus are the same ones which suggest that we can *know* him. Besides, historical questions aren't the *only* ones worth asking, are they?

For example, the Gospel of John records Jesus as praying this to his Father shortly before he was crucified:

> Father, the hour has come; glorify your Son that the Son may glorify you, since you have given him authority over all flesh, to give eternal life to all whom you have given him. And this is eternal life, that they know you the only true God, and Jesus Christ whom you have sent (17.1–3).

According to Jesus' own words, it *is* possible to know him and to know God as well, and this is what the whole business of "eternal life" is about: knowing who God really is by "seeing" him in the person of his Son, Jesus (John 1.14–18). And he wasn't talking only about those who were his contemporaries, since later in this prayer he prayed for "those who will believe in me" through the words of his disciples (17.20).

He's Still Here

John isn't the only New Testament author who suggests we can know Jesus today. At the beginning of his Gospel, Luke tells his patron Theophilus that it seemed good to him to "write an orderly account for you, most excellent Theophilus, that you may have certainty concerning the things you have been taught" (Luke 1.3–4). Later, in "Volume 2" of his work, the book of Acts, Luke continues in this vein: "In the first book, O Theophilus, I have dealt with all that Jesus began to do and teach, until the day when he was taken up, after he had given commands through the Holy Spirit to the apostles whom he had chosen" (Acts 1.1–2). Notice that Luke says the first book (the Gospel of Luke) was about what Jesus *"began* to do and teach." As far as Luke is concerned, the story isn't finished yet, because Jesus isn't finished yet. And so he goes ahead in Acts to describe what Jesus *continued* to do and teach through the presence of the Holy Spirit, his spiritual presence with his followers now that he has gone back into heaven (Acts 1.6–11). The first thing Luke records Jesus as saying to his disciples following his resurrection concerns the coming Holy Spirit, the "promise of the Father" which would come upon them very soon (Acts 1.4–5). And as we continue reading Acts, we learn what Jesus *continued* to do and teach through the presence of the Spirit with his people.

That being the case, it seems reasonable that the book of Acts would be a good place to look in order to answer our question: "Is it possible to know Jesus today?" And if so, how?

From "Knowing About" to "Knowing"

The coming of the Holy Spirit which Jesus had promised in Acts 1 becomes reality in the next chapter. It was the Jewish feast day of Pentecost (from the Greek word for "50," because it was celebrated 50 days after the Passover; and remember that Jesus was crucified at Passover). Jerusalem was swollen with pilgrims who had gathered in the city to celebrate the festival. The disciples of Jesus were there, too, just as he had told them to be, and suddenly they were caught up in three phenomena that signaled the Spirit's arrival. First, there was a sound like a powerful wind; second, the appearance of something that looked like fire above their heads; and third, the miraculous ability to speak in languages they had not learned (see 2.8 for the indication that these were actual languages), which they used to tell "the mighty works of God."

Naturally, all of this attracted a crowd who wanted to know what it was about. You see, the phenomena were not the main event of Pentecost, since they had to be interpreted. There was something more going on here, and Peter stood up to tell them what it was. He explained first of all that the prophet Joel had foretold the event they were witnessing several centuries before; it was the fulfillment of God's promise to one day "pour out" his Spirit on "all flesh," rather than just on prophets, kings, and other leaders of the Israelite people (2.14–21). Now this Spirit—the presence of Christ—would be available to all. But having explained that, Peter went immediately into a summary of Jesus, the mighty works God had done through him, how he had been delivered up to be crucified, and how death was not the end of his story. Peter claimed that God raised Jesus from the dead, a fact which he demonstrated through quotations of Psalms 16.8–11 and 110.1 (Acts 2.22–35). Here's the climax of his message: "Let all the house of Israel therefore know for certain that God has made him both Lord and Christ, this Jesus whom you crucified" (v 36).

Such a message must have been extremely troubling to those who heard Peter that day, especially since he was implicating them in the death of Jesus—not the messianic pretender they had taken him to be, but none other than God's Messiah and the Lord. So it isn't surprising that they immediately asked Peter and the other apostles, "What shall we do?" (v 37). Peter's answer was unequivocal and straight to the point: "Repent and be baptized every one of you in the name of Jesus Christ for the forgiveness of your sins, and you will receive the gift of the Holy Spirit" (v 38). Did you catch that? Peter said that those who repented and who were baptized in Jesus' name would *receive the Holy Spirit*. In other words, the presence of Christ would be with them, too. The Christ they had crucified was now the risen Christ, ever present with those who would believe in him and follow his teachings. Notice, too, that Peter's answer to their question tied them directly to the message about the historical Jesus; it was him in whom they needed to believe and whom they needed to obey. This is how they would "know" him, through the message about him and the presence of the Holy Spirit within them. Later, as groups other than Jews came to receive this same message, it was once again the Spirit's presence which signaled that they were acceptable to God (Samaritans [half-Jews] in 8.14–16; Gentiles in 10.44–48 and 11.15–18).

It is important to note that this receiving of the Holy Spirit comes as a direct result of hearing the message about the historical Jesus, believing it, and obeying it. This is emphasized in Acts 5.32, when Peter and the other apostles were brought before the Jewish authorities and threatened if they didn't stop talking about Jesus. They first replied, "We must obey God rather than men" (v 29), but then said, "And we are witnesses to these things, and so is the Holy Spirit, whom God has given to those who obey him." The Spirit (i.e., Jesus' presence) did not come merely from knowing about him, nor was it the product of an emotional experience. It resulted from accepting as true the message about Jesus that we have been exploring and from obeying what the apostles had commanded—repentance and baptism in Jesus' name. In saying this the apostles were merely doing what Jesus had earlier instructed them to do: "Go therefore and make disciples of all nations, baptizing them in the name of the Father and of the Son and of the Holy Spirit, teaching them to observe all that I have commanded you. And behold, *I am with you always*, to the end of the age" (Matt 28.19–20).

Paul, Meet Jesus

Earlier I pointed out that one of our most important historical sources of information about Jesus is Paul, who called himself the "apostle to the Gentiles" because he believed God had singled him out to take the story of Jesus to those outside the boundaries of Judaism (Acts 9.15; Rom 11.13; Gal 1.15–16; 2.9). When we first encounter Paul in the book of Acts, he is not "Paul the apostle," but Saul of Tarsus, a violent persecutor of the new Christian faith (by his own admission, Gal 1.13). As such, he did not know Jesus. But when Jesus appeared to him as he was on his way to persecute believers, Saul asked, "Who are you Lord?" and was told, "I am Jesus, whom you are persecuting" (Acts 9.5). It was three days before he understood what all of this meant for him, but a man named Ananias came to him and told him it was the Lord Jesus who had appeared to him and who had sent Ananias to lay hands on him so he could receive his sight and be filled with the Holy Spirit (Acts 9.17–18). As he later recounted these momentous events, Paul (as he comes to be called from Acts 13.13 on) recalled how Ananias had instructed him saying, "And now why do you wait? Rise and be baptized and wash away your sins, calling on his name" (Acts 22.16). And that's how Paul came to know Jesus.

But knowing Jesus wasn't over for Paul. In a very interesting passage in his letter to the Christians in the Greek city of Philippi, he indicates that knowing Jesus was something he had already experienced but also something he desired to do more and more. Paul's words occur in the context of a warning to the Philippian Christians to avoid people who tried to tell them that just following Jesus wasn't enough, that they needed to add the Jewish law to the message of Christ—specifically, that they needed to be circumcised. (This was a common problem in the earliest days of Christianity. See Acts 15.1–5; Gal 5.1–6.) After demonstrating in Philippians 3.4–6 that he was "as Jewish as anybody," Paul wrote this:

> But whatever gain I had, I counted as loss for the sake of Christ. Indeed, I count everything as loss because of the surpassing worth of knowing Christ Jesus my Lord. For his sake I have suffered the loss of all things and count them as rubbish, in order that I may gain Christ and be found in him, not having a righteousness of my own that comes from the law, but that which comes through faith in Christ, the righteousness from God that depends on faith—that I may know him and the power of his resurrection, and may share his sufferings, becoming like him in his death, that by any means possible I may attain the resurrection from the dead. Not that I have already obtained this or am already perfect, but I press on to make it my own, because Christ Jesus has made me his own. (Phil 3.7–12)

Notice that Paul says both that he already knew Christ and that he desired to know Christ more. He seems to have thought of knowing Christ as both present experience and as a goal which he continually pursued. It wasn't simply knowledge *about* Christ that Paul desired (after all, he had already seen him; see 1 Cor 9.1), but knowledge *of Christ*. And he indicates that this greater knowledge of his Lord would come through becoming more and more like him, especially as he shared in Jesus' own sufferings by continuing to spread the good news about him, which was often a costly endeavor (see Phil 1.12–30).

An On-Going Relationship

As we have seen in the example of Paul, meeting Jesus isn't a one-time thing. It isn't something that happens to us and then we just walk away from it. How could we? Who would want to? But there are implications of knowing Jesus—life-changing implications.

When John wrote his first letter toward the end of the First Century AD, he was writing to a group of Christians who had experienced a tragic conflict with other believers who were denying that Jesus and the Christ were the same being (similar to the Gnostics we discussed in Chapter Two). Also, these opponents of the church were abandoning the way of life taught by Jesus and had slid into an immoral lifestyle. As a result, John says, they *didn't* know Jesus.

> This is the message we have heard from him and proclaim to you, that God is light, and in him is no darkness at all. If we say we have fellowship with him while we walk in darkness, we lie and do not practice the truth. But if we walk in the light as he is in the light, we have fellowship with one another, and the blood of Jesus his Son cleanses us from all sin… And by this we know that we have come to know him, if we keep his commandments. Whoever says "I know him" but does not keep his commandments is a liar, and the truth is not in him… (1 John 1.5–8; 2.4)

According to John, as for Paul, knowing Jesus means walking as he walked (lived) and as he taught his followers to live (2.6). This means that "knowing Jesus" isn't just about having certain feelings about him or being privy to some mystical knowledge, but it's living in his presence in the way that he directs. And the directions are found in the New Testament documents such as 1 John, the letters of Paul, and the Gospels, the same documents that tell us about Jesus himself.

A Never-Ending Knowledge

Jesus also promised that our relationship with him does not end with our experiences of this life. Rather, he said that when we know him, we belong to him, and he will eventually return and claim us as his own to be with him forever. To the disciples who were deeply troubled at the thought of his departure (death), Jesus said, "Let not your hearts be troubled. Believe in God; believe also in me. In my Father's house are many rooms. If it were not so, would I have told you that I go and prepare a place for you? And if I go and prepare a place for you, I will come again and will take you to myself, that where I am you may be also" (John 14.1–3). When one of them, Thomas, complained of not knowing the way where Jesus was going, he replied, "I am the way, and the truth, and the life" (14.6). We need not have the ability to decipher a complicated set of instructions to be with Jesus; we need only to follow him.

So the New Testament indicates that it is possible to know Jesus, and not just to know about him. We know him through the message of his life, death, and resurrection; we know him through our obedient response to that message in the acts of repentance and baptism; we know him through his Spirit who comes to live within us; and we know him by living as he taught and as he himself lived. And knowing him, we can live with him forever.

A word of caution: We have already seen that those who knew Jesus and followed him in the First Century were changed dramatically by their experience. So we have every reason to believe that we, too, will be changed—indeed, that we need to be and ought to be. Knowing Jesus will not leave you the same as before.

Are you ready to meet him?

Annotated Bibliography

Note: The number of books on Jesus is incredibly large, even counting only fairly recent ones. No attempt has been made to give anything like a complete listing, only those which are readily accessible and which will offer the interested reader a place to go for further information on the various topics related to Jesus.

Barnett, Paul. *Is the New Testament Reliable?* 2nd ed. InterVarsity, 2005. A recent treatment of the subject which covers much of the same ground as the classic work by F. F. Bruce (see below).

Barrett, C. K., ed. *The New Testament Background: Writings from Ancient Greece and the Roman Empire That Illuminate Christian Origins.* rev. ed. HarperSanFrancisco, 1995. A standard collection of ancient texts that allow modern readers to read the original sources for themselves.

Bock, Darrell L. *The Missing Gospels: Unearthing the Truth Behind Alternative Christianities.* Nelson, 2006. Challenges the claim that the Gnostic gospels show that Christianity was, from its beginnings, a movement containing diverse views of Jesus.

Bruce, F. F. *The New Testament Documents: Are They Reliable?* 6th ed. Eerdmans, 1981. A brief discussion which has gone through many editions and re-printings, designed for the general reader. An excellent beginning point for those interested in this question.

Charlesworth, J. H. *Jesus and the Dead Sea Scrolls.* Doubleday, 1992. A world-class authority on the Dead Sea Scrolls challenges the view that Jesus was an Essene and that the Dead Sea Scrolls are an important source for understanding his identity.

Copan, Paul, ed. *Will the Real Jesus Please Stand Up? A Debate Between William Lane Craig and John Dominic Crossan.* Baker, 1998. A dialogue between leading scholars with opposite views of Jesus.

Crossan, John Dominic. *Jesus: A Revolutionary Biography.* HarperSanFrancisco, 1995. Contains Crossan's arguments for his claim that Jesus' body was not buried as the Gospels report.

—————. *The Historical Jesus: The Life of a Mediterranean Jewish Peasant.* HarperSanFrancisco, 1991. A leading member of the Jesus Seminar presents a view of Jesus quite different from that found in the Gospels.

Dowley, Tim. *Kregel Bible Atlas.* Kregel, 2002. A good basic atlas containing excellent maps and a brief but helpful text. Useful for locating the ministry of Jesus in the context of Israel's historical development, as well as the eventual spread of Christianity in that region.

Dunn, James D. G. *A New Perspective on Jesus: What the Quest for the Historical Jesus Missed.* Baker Academic, 2005. An eminent British scholar points out the fallacies of many of the assumptions which dominate Jesus studies today and argues that the best explanation for what we have in the Gospels is the actual life of Jesus.

Evans, Craig A. *Fabricating Jesus: How Modern Scholars Distort the Gospels.* IVP, 2006. Detailed discussion of the methodologies and presuppositions of much of current scholarship that lead to negative conclusions about the historical reliability of the Gospels.

Ferguson, Everett. *Backgrounds of Early Christianity.* 3rd ed. Eerdmans, 2003. A very useful and reliable introduction to the Jewish and Greco-Roman backgrounds of the New Testament.

Funk, Robert W. *Honest to Jesus.* HarperSanFrancisco, 1996. One of the leaders of the Jesus Seminar sets forth his desire to "rescue Jesus" from the traditional Christian understanding of him.

Geisler, Norman L. and Paul K. Hoffman, eds. *Why I Am a Christian: Leading Thinkers Explain Why They Believe.* rev. and exp ed. Baker, 2006. A collection of essays by leading Christian thinkers, explaining why they believe and what they believe about Jesus, Christian faith, and the Bible.

Metzger, Bruce M. *The New Testament: Its Background, Growth, and Content.* 3rd ed. Abingdon, 2003. An older but still very reliable guide to the contents and development of the New Testament. An excellent starting point for those just beginning to inquire into this subject.

Mountcastle, William M. *The Secret Ministry of Jesus: Pioneer Prophet of Interfaith Dialogue.* University Press of America, 2007. A recent statement of claims that Jesus traveled widely to such faraway places as Tibet.

Wells, G. A. "Earliest Christianity." *The New Humanist*, vol. 114, no. 3, 13–18. September, 1999. Along with the two works cited below, Wells states his case that Jesus never existed.

——————. *The Jesus Myth.* Open Court, 1998.

——————. *The Jesus Legend.* Open Court, 1996.

Witherington, Ben III. *What Have They Done With Jesus? Beyond Strange Theories and Bad History.* A leading American historian and biblical scholar exposes the distortions of Jesus that result from poor historical methodologies.

Wright, N. T. *The Challenge of Jesus: Rediscovering Who Jesus Was and Is.* IVP Academic, 1999. Examines the Jewish setting of Jesus' life, the nature of his mission, the question of the historicity of the resurrection, and the relation of the historical Jesus to the desire to follow him today.

More about Jesus
By Craig B. Manning

Jesus and His Parables

The parables of Jesus provide a wonderfully unique view of the kingdom of heaven. This is one of the very few books that, in addition to examining the words of Jesus, explore the first century world of Jesus to gain insight into the parables. His narratives telling of the kingdom were based on the historical, political, and cultural world of His day. This book bridges the 2,000 year gap between now and the time of Jesus to help understand the kingdom of heaven as revealed in the parables. 284 pages. $13.99 (PB)

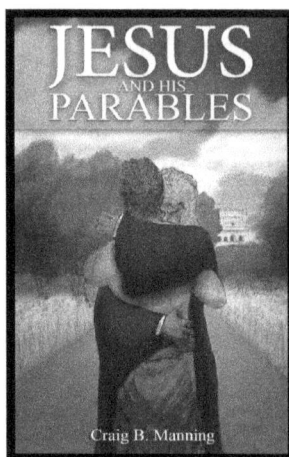

"*Jesus and His Parables* helps contemporary readers to bridge the gap between our world and the original world of the parables by attending to the Jewish world of the first century of the Christian Era and to the history of scholarship on the parables. ...Readers will find in this volume help from one who trusts the Scriptures and seeks the texts' transforming message."

W. H. Bellinger, Jr.
Chair, Department of Religion
W. Marshall and Lulie Craig Chairholder in Bible
Baylor University

"With one foot squarely in the church and its interpretive traditions and the other planted in modern scholarly trends, Manning moves methodically through various parables with impressive skill and deference to the many ways the parables have shaped Christian communities."

David B. Capes
Thomas Nelson Research Professor
Houston Baptist University

More about Jesus
By Paul Earnhart

Invitation to a Spiritual Revolution
Studies in the Sermon on the Mount

Few preachers have studied the Sermon on the Mount as intensively or spoken on its contents so frequently and effectively as the author of this work. His excellent and very readable written analysis appeared first as a series of articles in *Christianity Magazine*. By popular demand it is here offered in one volume so that it can be more easily preserved, circulated, read, reread and made available to those who would not otherwise have access to it. Foreword by Sewell Hall. 173 pages. $9.99 (PB)

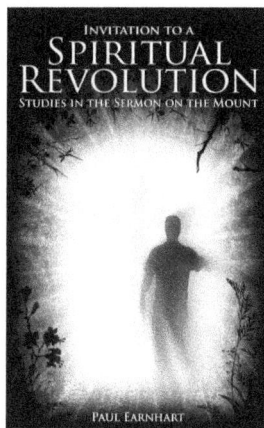

Glimpses of Eternity
Studies in the Parables of Jesus

The parables of Jesus are the compelling stories and illustrations from our familiar world which the Lord used to open windows for us into heaven. They help us to understand the heart of God and the nature of the spiritual kingdom which His Son has brought into the world at such an awful cost. There are messages of comfort in the parables and some stern warnings too. They are best understood by those who have a longing to know God's Son and to follow Him in genuine earnestness. These studies are the compilation of a series of articles written for *Christianity Magazine*. 198 pages. $11.99 (PB)

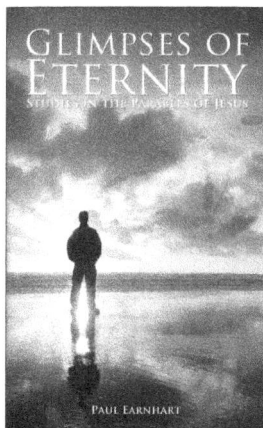

Also from DeWard

Beneath the Cross: Essays and Relfections on the Lord's Supper
Jady S. Copeland and Nathan Ward (editors)

The Bible has much to say about the Lord's Supper. Almost every component of this memorial is rich with meaning—meaning supplied by Old Testament foreshadowing and New Testament teaching. The Lord's death itself is meaningful and significant in ways we rarely point out. In sixty-nine essays by forty different authors, Beneath the Cross explores the depths of symbolism and meaning to be found in the last hours of the Lord's life and offers a helpful look at the memorial feast that commemorates it. 329 pages. $14.99 (PB); $23.99 (HB)

The Man of Galilee
Atticus G. Haygood

Haygood's argument for the deity of Christ simply from the presentation of Jesus given in the Gospels: Jesus Himself as evidence for His deity. This short book gives a thoughtful, thorough, and logical presentation of the unique and universal quality of the character of Jesus. 108 pages. $8.99 (PB)

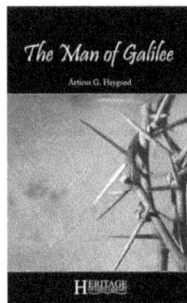

The Slave of Christ
Seth Parr

Immerse yourself in a place where sacrifice is reasonable, love and action are sensible, victory is guaranteed, and evangelism explodes. While the sacrifice of Jesus opens the door for us to Heaven, we must work to be conformed into His very image. In The Slave of Christ, uncover what biblical service means and how it can change your life. Energize your spiritual walk and awaken the servant within. 96 pages. $8.99 (PB)

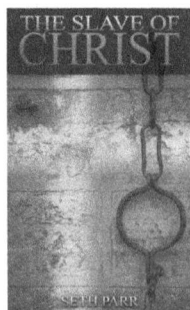

HERITAGE
OF FAITH LIBRARY

The **DeWard Publishing Company Heritage of Faith Library** is a growing collection of classic Christian reprints. DeWard has already published or has plans to publish the following authors:

- A. B. Bruce
- Atticus G. Haygood
- H. C. Leupold
- J. W. McGarvey
- William Paley
- Albertus Pieters
- B. F. Westcott

Future authors and titles added to this series will be announced on our website.

For a full listing of DeWard Publishing Company books, visit our website:

www.deward.com

DEWARD
PUBLISHING COMPANY